P9-CLD-275

THE GOD CATCHERS

OTHER BOOKS BY TOMMY TENNEY

The God Chasers

God's Favorite House

God's Dream Team

God's Secret to Greatness
(with David Cape)

Secret Sources of Power
(with T. F. Tenney)

THE GOD CATCHERS

EXPERIENCING THE MANIFEST PRESENCE OF GOD

TOMMY TENNEY

THOMAS NELSON PUBLISHERS®
Nashville

Copyright © 2000 by Tommy Tenney

All rights reserved. Written permission must be secured from the publisher to use or reproduce any part of this book, except for brief quotations in critical reviews or articles.

Published in Nashville, Tennessee, by Thomas Nelson, Inc.

Unless otherwise noted, Scripture quotations are from THE NEW KING JAMES VERSION. Copyright © 1979, 1980, 1982, Thomas Nelson, Inc., Publishers.

Scripture quotations noted KJV are from the KING JAMES VERSION of the Bible.

Cover Design: Uttley/DouPonce DesignWorks

Library of Congress Cataloging-in-Publication Data
Tenney, Tommy, 1956–
    The God catchers : experiencing the manifest presence of God / Tommy Tenney.
        p. cm.
    ISBN 0-7852-6710-7
    1. Spiritual life—Christianity. I. Title.
BV4501.3 .T46 2001
248—dc21   00-067563
                                                                CIP

Printed in the United States of America
5 6 7 8 BVG 06 05 04 03 02 01

This book is dedicated to the GodChasers.network staff. This tireless team has chased God and kept pace with me through good times and bad. They caught the vision and carried the burden for many an extra mile. God brought them all here, and no one could ask for a better collection of giftings, wisdom, and passion.

We've come a long way, but I will never forget where we began. My original "staff" was my family—my loving wife and three beautiful daughters, to whom I also dedicate this book. There is no way to overstate the importance of their love and support. They "hold up my arms" when I am weary, and they give me refuge from the battle.

CONTENTS

THE GOD CATCHERS

I

DOES GOD PLAY HIDE-AND-SEEK?

THINGS I WISH I KNEW THE DAY I NEARLY CAUGHT HIM

HAVE YOU EVER WONDERED WHY IT SOMETIMES FEELS as if God is hiding from you? I know I've felt that way sometimes. Perhaps that is why He launched me on a journey of His own choosing when He interrupted my self-defined successful career as a full-time evangelist with a simple but shocking revelation: *You know, Tommy, your favorite services and My favorite services are not the same. You leave your services full and satisfied, but when you leave, I'm still hungry.*

God whispered this to me during a life-changing early Sunday morning service. It was a divine encounter that forever imprinted itself with indelible ink on the pages of my memory. In a way, I could almost identify with how Isaiah felt the day he suddenly saw God "high and lifted up" in the temple long ago.[1]

There were tears in my eyes when I whispered to my wife, "I don't think I've ever been this close to Him before." Hundreds of other people who were in the building that day will testify to the same sensation. It was as if we "caught" Him.

I wish I knew then what I have discerned since—that God will leave our meetings full and satisfied only when we begin to leave them feeling hungrier for Him than when we first came.

The Lord began to teach me about the importance of being a *God Chaser* during a nine-month period of what I call "divine discontent." It culminated in an encounter with Him—an encounter from which I have never recovered.

Now I am no longer content just to "chase" Him. I want to "catch" Him, to collect a string of close encounters with Him. Sometimes I grow weary with the daily chase, but I must chase if I want to catch.

During that period of growing discontent, God planted in my heart the seeds for a book titled *The God Chasers*. I had no idea that book would ignite such a firestorm of hunger for God. I knew only how hungry I was.

My desire to sustain the collected moments with God made me feel the frustration of Jacob: "If I ever get my hands on Him, I'll not let go." And there is where I discovered another piece to the puzzle of His presence— and the message for this book—only this time it came while I was hiding behind a closet door.

God used my youngest daughter to teach me about Himself once again. Class began with the sound of her little bare feet padding across the linoleum floor and the sight of her irresistible smile as she said, "Let's play hidey-face, Daddy!"

I'm sure you played similar games with your children. I played hidey-face with all my girls. My most recent play partner was my youngest daughter, so my memories of her joyful discoveries during the hidey-face game are the freshest.

> Every minute seemed like an hour for me because I was waiting for the joy of our encounter.

My memories began when she still wore those oversized plastic-coated disposable diapers that made a telltale *whoosh-whoosh* sound every time she walked. I tracked her every step as she looked for me in all the strange places that seem so logical from a toddler's point of view. I listened from my hiding place behind the closet door as she looked for me in the oven, in the trash bin, and in the ridiculously crowded space under the kitchen sink.

With growing anticipation I listened to my little pursuer's every move because I had a plan in mind. Every minute seemed like an hour for me

because I was waiting for the joy of our encounter. I could barely wait to see her face light up the moment she discovered her long-lost daddy.

If it was clear that my petite pursuer was having trouble finding me, then I would be careful to leave something showing to help her along. If I was behind the closet door, then I'd make sure part of my foot was showing. If I took refuge behind the couch, then I'd make sure that just enough of my backside showed to help her find me.

Why be so careful? It is simple: the point of our elaborate game of hidey-face wasn't the hiding; *it was the finding!* I wasn't hiding from my little girl so that she couldn't find me; I was careful to hide so that she *could* find me.

Then I remembered that God did the same thing with Moses. If you recall, He was careful to leave part of His divine "backside" showing so Moses could see Him. Evidently Moses was a lot like my daughter because he wasn't satisfied with that. He wanted more. He wanted to see God's face; he longed to see His glory.

WE COME TO CHURCH FOR DIFFERENT REASONS THAN GOD DOES

I've continued to learn more about the pursuit of His presence since I first started chasing Him. I wish I had known these things the day I "almost caught Him."

I've learned more about the fuel of desperation and the feel of destiny while in pursuit of His presence. The Lord also taught me more about embracing the place of what I previously called a "frustrating funk, a divine depression of destiny."[2] Weariness with man can birth desperation for God.

Even then I had hints in my heart that, in some supernatural way, the pursuer becomes the pursued when God catches wind of our worship and praise. I was beginning to understand the power of collective hunger where corporate visitations of God were concerned.

Isaiah's vision of God in the sixth chapter of his prophetic book occupied a prominent place in my early understanding of the way God revealed His manifest presence to men. The Holy Spirit has opened my eyes to see this same scripture passage from a totally new viewpoint—one that has everything to do with catching God, so to speak.

I didn't realize it at the time, but I was speaking prophetically of this book when I wrote about that encounter with God's manifest presence in *The God Chasers:*

> The instant Isaiah the prophet, the chosen servant of God, saw the King of glory, what he used to think was clean and holy now looked like filthy rags. He was thinking, *I thought I knew God, but I didn't know **this much** of God!* That Sunday we seemed to come so close; we almost caught Him. Now I know it's possible.[3]

If you can get that close, you can catch Him! Often, when we wander off in the wrong direction in our pursuit of Him, God calls out to us to help us along. When my youngest daughter and I played hidey-face, I loved to hear the lyrical sounds of her "little girl giggle" just bubbling with excitement. I loved it so much that if she wandered off in the wrong direction and stopped giggling in her search, then I would call out and say, "Over here . . . closer . . ."

Then I would listen to her stop and *be still* while she tried to locate the source of Daddy's voice. *I am convinced that God does the same thing.*

One day a young man named Samuel was searching for Him, and evidently he got really close to where God was hiding. When he failed to find Him, God whispered, "Samuel . . ."

Then God's young pursuer promptly went running in the wrong direction as we often do! In our immaturity, we often chase after man's voice thinking it is God's voice. Only repeated attempts by God and truth from ministers can help us locate the source of that "still small voice."

God keeps trying. Perhaps now it is time for the ministry to say, "It's not *us* . . . even if you hear Him through our voices . . . it's not us." Respond to Him! Speak to Him!

"Eli, was that you?"

"No, that wasn't me."

"Samuel . . ."

What was about to happen? *A God Chaser was about to become a God Catcher.* Even elderly Eli had "cornered" God a few times. He said, "Samuel, let me tell you how to respond the next time you hear that voice." Then he taught Samuel the simple but profound process by which you capture God in that moment of divine encounter.

At least eleven times in the Psalms, David said in effect, "You are a God who hides Himself . . ."⁴ Why would the God of the universe, the almighty Creator, hide Himself from His creation? We know, for instance, that He hides Himself from sin and pride, basically because He doesn't want His absolute holiness to destroy us in our pollution. But that isn't the main reason that God hides. He sent His only Son to take care of the sin problem forever once we repent and turn to Him. I think the biblical answer has more to do with joy than with judgment.

> At least eleven times in the Psalms, David said, in effect, "You are a God who hides Himself . . ."

I often tell the story of the years when my youngest daughter was still riding a big yellow bus to school each day. She's reached that "grown-up little girl stage" now where she doesn't like to ride buses anymore because "they're hot and sweaty," but I miss the joyful encounters I had with her when that bus rolled up to our driveway.

At the end of a long ministry trip, I began to miss her and her older sisters so much that I'd skip sleep and take an early flight just so I could beat them home from school.

Some of the greatest highlights in my memories are those afternoons when I could sneak home early so I could be standing in the driveway when the school bus pulled up.

I love to pass through the treasured mental snapshots of my girls growing up, and some of the best close-ups I remember come from those precious moments of joyful reunion in the driveway.

The pursuit and "capture" of God is a process. When my youngest daughter stepped off that yellow school bus, she went through a very similar process with me. I can still see it in my mind. She stepped off the bus surrounded by all her little buddies, talking a mile a minute, with her sweater dragging on the ground and one shoe untied. (That's why sweaters last only one year—when little kids get off the school bus, they drag them along behind with their backpacks.)

I lived for the moment her eyes found me. Suddenly she forgot everything around her except for one thing: "Daddy! Daddy! Daddy!" After three short steps, the sweater was on the ground, followed by the backpack three steps later. Then I had to brace myself because I knew she was going to launch herself at me in a desperate lunge of love.

The scene that captures my mind is the look of sheer excitement on her face. I had surprised her, and she was overjoyed. She knew I was coming home, but I met her early when she least expected it.

She was immersed in the liquid joy of discovery and delighted by the unexpected excitement and serendipitous moment of encounter, *"It's him!"* Then we enjoyed about thirty seconds of sheer pleasure as we went through our private process of rediscovery and delight.

First she would jump into my arms. After a crushing hug I had to swing her around and around in a circle with her feet flying in the air while she laughed and giggled uncontrollably. When I finally set her down, she wanted to kiss me again.

At that point, I would usually turn away. "Why?" you may ask. "Didn't you want to be kissed?" Of course, I did, but I knew that if I turned away, it would make my little girl pursue me even harder and she would give me even more kisses. It was a very well-organized plot. *I didn't run away*—I turned away. God doesn't leave either—He lingers. His greatest joy is to extend and expand the moments of encounter. Sunday morning kisses are not enough!

The moment I turned away from my little girl, she would get "the look" on her face and start the process again by saying with all the determination she could muster: "I'm going to kiss you, Daddy!"

"No, you're not kissing me. Look at you. You are all dirty! You've got mud all over you—you're not kissing me!"

"I'm going to kiss you, Daddy! I'm going to kiss you."

"No, you're not kissing me."

> God doesn't leave either—He lingers. His greatest joy is to extend and expand the moments of encounter. Sunday morning kisses are not enough!

And so the game began again. She was determined to kiss me, but it wasn't hard for me to avoid her. I could easily move my two-hundred-and-none-of-your-business pounds this way and that way to dodge her.

Within a few minutes, she would get tired and say, "Oh, Daddy," and stop her pursuit. She couldn't capture me physically, but she easily captured me emotionally. She couldn't move her legs fast enough to apprehend me, but her words easily captured my heart.

Some people take offense at my use of the term *God Chaser*, saying, "You don't have to chase God." I understand but I don't agree. You may call it whatever you want; it doesn't bother me. My youngest daughter didn't have to chase me to get me to be her daddy, but if she wanted more than just to live in the same house, if she wanted attention and affection, then she knew which "buttons" to push. You may be content just to be in God's house, but I want to be in His lap!

I do agree that none of us can ever really catch Him. That much is obvious. His ways are as far removed from our ways as the east is from the west. None of us can catch Him through physical effort, mental gymnastics, or passionless spiritual exertion. "Works" can't catch Him, but an appeal to mercy and grace . . . !

The "catching" will come if you can ever get to that point of weary desperation where you just say, "Oh, Daddy!" All of a sudden, you capture and enrapture the heart of the God you can't take captive any other way. The One you are chasing will suddenly become the One who pursues you!

If You Are a Worshiper, God Will Track You Down!

At the very moment my little daughter would say, "Oh, Daddy," I would turn and begin to chase her. Worship turns the tables on the chase. It takes you to the point where you don't have to pursue Him because He begins to pursue you. If you are a worshiper, *God will track you down.* He will find you even if you are left in the bottom of a Philippian prison with your hands in chains as Paul and Silas were. If you are a worshiper, He will track you down and seek you out.

It is as if He stands up in heaven and says:

> "I smell worship."
> "Where is it coming from, God?"
> "I don't know, but I'm going to find it right now."

Worship and spiritual hunger make you so attractive to God that your circumstances cease to matter anymore. He will move heaven and earth to find a worshiper. When you begin to worship with all your being and desire, your heart turns Him toward you. You capture His attention and attract His affection.

It transforms you from being a God Chaser to the potential of being a God Catcher. Your worship essentially sets a "lover's entrapment" for Him. If the Song of Solomon is any indication, then this kind of "passionate entrapment" is His delight.

Let me return to the simple illustration of a father playing with his children. It is nearly impossible to get my adolescent daughters to play hidey-face with me anymore. When they were newborns, all I had to do was smile, and they would gurgle with excitement. Then I moved up to the more advanced game of hiding my eyes with my hand. I could keep them laughing, cooing, and gurgling almost endlessly with that simple act of hiding and finding again.

Ultimately they moved to greater independence when they began to walk and our game involved more separation and much more seeking, but it still ended in a riotous reunion marked by the joy of fresh encounter. My three daughters have nearly outgrown the game of hidey-face now, so I have to seek out the two-year-old children of my assistants because they are still at that age of joyful discovery.

> Spiritual conversion mixed with childlike wonder is irresistible to God.

It is normal for children to grow up, but God defines another kind of *normal* for His kingdom. The only way to understand what I'm talking about is to become like a little child. I think I read that somewhere too. Did you read the same Book? "Unless you are converted and become as little children, you will by no means enter the kingdom of heaven."[5] Spiritual conversion mixed with childlike wonder is irresistible to God.

As I said, when my children were little, I would often hide from them. Yet the hiding wasn't the purpose of the whole game. The joy of finding and being found was the purpose of the game. *The hiding was just something I had to do to create the moment that I wanted.*

I thought nothing of waking up at four o'clock in the morning after ministering in a long evening service and enduring six to eight hours in airports and on the plane just so I could experience thirty seconds of my daughter's joy in the driveway. Of course, five minutes later she was ready to play with the kids in the neighborhood. Even so, it was worth it for me to be there to see her. That was the whole purpose. *It was worth it.* God will take a trip in time just to spend a brief moment with humanity. He thinks it's worth it to be with you!

God loves it when you discover Him, but how can you discover Him if He doesn't sometimes hide? The Scriptures are full of examples showing that God "hides." The Bible records, "Seek My face," and "Seek the LORD while He may be found."[6] The most important thing I've learned, and the most important point in this book, is this:

God doesn't hide Himself from you so that He *can't* be found; He hides Himself from you so that He *can* be found. He hides for the sheer joy of being discovered.

Even though my youngest daughter has partially outgrown the hidey-face game, I can still manage to squeeze some great kisses and hugs from her if I really work at it. The other day I said, "Honey, come up here and give Daddy some love. Give me some kisses."

She was busy playing with some of her dolls and things, but she obediently crawled up on my lap and gave me a kiss. Then she was ready to get down again.

"No, come on. Give me some more love," I said.

Then she said, "That's the problem with you daddies."

> God doesn't hide Himself from you so that He *can't* be found; He hides Himself from you so that He *can* be found.

"What do you mean?" I said.

"You always want too much love," she said.

I could only grin and say, "Yeah, I'm guilty."

That's the problem with our Daddy too: *He always wants too much love.* We give Him a perfunctory kiss on Sunday morning and hurry to return to our religious toys and pretend encounters. All the while He is saying, "I've been missing you; I'd love to have some more loving kisses and hugs from you."

God loves it when we want to linger in His presence, but those times are rare in most modern churches. We've become more time sensitive than Spirit sensitive. Whatever happened to "waiting on God"?

This book has one simple and straightforward focus: *how you can capture God's heart.* It's not that you must run faster to catch God, because you can never run fast enough to overtake Him. However, if you pursue His heart in passionate hunger, your words of desperation have the power to capture and "corner" His heart. In that moment, the Pursued becomes the Pursuer and the God Chaser becomes the God Catcher.

As a father, I am constantly conniving to squeeze just one more hug or kiss from the daughters I love so much. I suspect our heavenly Father does the same. Our problem in the church is that if we are not careful, the arrogance of our spiritual adolescence robs us of our childlike passion for His presence. More than anything else, we must learn that *God does not hide so that He* cannot *be found; He is very careful to hide so that He* can *be found.*

2

BURNING LIPS AND HOT HEARTS

SOMEBODY CAUGHT HIM:
THE TRUE STORY OF A GOD CATCHER

A RE YOU PART OF THE "RESTLESS REMNANT" THAT IS incurably desperate for an encounter with God?[1] The symptoms are unmistakable. Your compulsive addiction for God makes you sick of church games, man's manipulation, and passionless worship services consisting of religious stage gymnastics and emotional hype designed to excite and stroke the flesh.

What happens when God Chasers "corner God"? When you finally get to the place of encounter, how do you stretch out that time of interaction and intimacy with divinity? How do you capture Him?

It should be obvious that no one can really "catch" God, but you can capture His heart. Once you do that, God allows you to pull Him into your dimension. Most of us don't realize it, but we do things like that all the time without even thinking about it. For instance, my daughters often come inside the house to seek my help or advice on things with routine requests like, "Daddy, I skinned my knee. Daddy, I'm thirsty. Daddy, will you play with me?"

Then there are other times when I hear their cry *outside* the house. My two younger daughters like to flit around the neighborhood on those new silver scooters with the little tiny wheels. (I was told they were the latest rage.) As a responsible parent, I try to make them wear helmets and elbow and kneepads, but kids are bound and determined to break the rules from time to time. That means it is inevitable that some skinned knees will come their way.

One day while I was sitting in the house I heard a bloodcurdling scream outside. Do you know what it's like to hear a scream and *know* that it belongs to your own child? For the first thirty seconds until you can get to the door, you have no idea whether she was hit by a Mack truck or bitten by a rabid Norwegian wolfhound.

THERE WAS AN URGENCY TO HER CRY

I threw down the papers I was working on, jumped up, and ran outside. My heart was pumping double time in an adrenaline rush by the time I discovered that my youngest daughter had fallen down and skinned her knee a little bit. How did that little girl physically pull my two-hundred-and-none-of-your-business pounds up from my place of thoughtful repose and transport me into her world as fast as my legs could carry me? Was it the strength of her little arms and delicate hands that did it? No, that is a physical and mathematical impossibility. She did it with her voice. There was an *urgency* to her cry.

Remember that God is not hiding so that He *can't* be found. He is very careful to hide so that He *can* be found. He *wants* you to find Him. Apparently the Old Testament prophet stumbled across God in the temple "before He had hidden Himself properly":

> In the year that King Uzziah died, I saw the Lord sitting on a throne, high and lifted up, and the train of His robe filled the temple.[2]

How many times did this prophet walk into the temple before that unforgettable day when he "caught" God? Isaiah wasn't the oldest or the most seasoned prophet alive in Judah that day, but he was the only one who saw the Lord "high and lifted up."

Isaiah's ministry spanned a period of forty years and the reign of as many as five different kings, but none of them equaled King Uzziah.[3] It is no wonder Isaiah had an encounter with God in the temple—he was just coming back from King Uzziah's funeral. He was still mourning the loss of one of Judah's few good kings, a man whose unlimited potential was tragically cut short through pride and religious presumption. Isaiah's grief might have been worse than we know because, according to rabbinic tradition, Isaiah was the first cousin of King Uzziah.[4]

ISAIAH WAS MOURNING OVER JUDAH'S "LEPER KING"

King Uzziah reigned in Jerusalem for fifty-two years beginning in his sixteenth year, and he is ranked as one of Judah's greatest "good kings." Uzziah managed to return Judah to a measure of her former glory under King David and King Solomon. Yet he isn't remembered for his great accomplishments; he is remembered for his great fall and ultimate death as a royal leper.[5]

None of us have room for two kings in our lives. It was only after King Uzziah finally died that the "other King" could rise up and say to Isaiah, "Now I'll let you see Me. You thought the glory of the former king was incredible; let Me show you My glory." The prophet wrote, "And his train filled the temple."[6]

Something happened to Isaiah that day that changed him forever. The prophet had prophesied to his nation long before his divine encounter in the temple, but after he caught sight of God taking His seat, Isaiah didn't see things the same way. He didn't say things the same way, and he didn't prophesy the same way.

What happened? Isaiah spent thirty seconds in the presence of the King, high and lifted up, and it utterly redirected, reformed, and transformed his life and ministry.[7]

Paul said, "He is not far from each one of us."[8] He's not hiding far from us, but how many times have we said to Him, "Oh, Lord . . . it's just You"? Forgive us for the arrogance of adolescence, Lord Jesus. We're desperate for You now. We are like little children begging You, "Do it again, Daddy. Show us Your Face."

Sometimes my children come into my home because they have the "keys" to the door; they understand how to make an entrance as members of the family. Then there are times when their cries pull me from my world into their world. In that respect, they capture me by capturing my attention. Worship captures the attention of God, but it "pulls Him into our world" *when the circumstances are just right.*

When the weather conditions are just right, when the humidity is at the perfect percentage, and the inside and outside temperatures are at certain points, frost will appear on your window. It doesn't happen all the time, *only when specific conditions are met.* I'm thinking that worship works the same way.

Have you ever looked closely at the frost that appears on a window on a cold winter day? The frost is comprised of thousands or millions of ice crystals formed from the moisture in the air. Each crystal has a totally unique design, and these designs interlock with each other to form what looks like manufactured crystalline snowflakes on the glass.

There is a real key revealed in this phenomenon of the natural realm: the design of that crystallized water in the form of frost has always *existed in another dimension.* We simply cannot see it until certain conditions are met that pull it into our sight. One source describes what scientists have discovered about the universal characteristics of frost patterns everywhere in the world:

> These beautiful forms have existed forever out in invisible space, just waiting for a cool windowpane and a cold day to bring them into visibility . . .
>
> These patterns are not exclusive to one land— they appear in all lands. They exist somewhere in

Forgive us for the arrogance of adolescence, Lord Jesus. We're desperate for You now. We are like little children begging You, "Do it again, Daddy. Show us Your face."

the infinite treasuries of God and are instantly available anywhere conditions are in alignment to bring them forth.[9]

All the components for the "frost recipe" are already present at any given time, but they exist "in another dimension" until certain conditions are met. In that moment, a bridge or gateway appears between the unseen world and the visible realm that allows you to see into the world of crystalline structures.

Have you ever seen or handled a piece of quartz crystal? If you could examine the molecular structure of that crystal, we know from scientific research that you would see a particular structure and order in each molecule of that crystal. They exist because the right environment existed for them to grow in the natural realm.

We must understand that God is always "there" in the sense that He is omnipresent, and we know from His Word and from the historical record of human encounters with Him that He tends to move and act in somewhat predictable patterns. However, you can't perceive or "see" Him until you create the proper climate and the right atmosphere. Suddenly God seems to appear from nowhere, but in reality He is always there. The principles and laws governing His presence are constant. The problem isn't that God is "missing"; the problem is that you must get hot enough. Create the atmosphere!

> The problem isn't that God is "missing"; the problem is that you must get hot enough.

Crystals appear to the natural eye only in the presence of the correct temperature gradient difference. Only a temperature change meeting certain conditions in the spirit realm will suddenly allow the "crystalline presence of God" to show up. In that moment, "something that was always there but in another dimension" will move into your world. I call it visitation, the "suddenly of God."

Worship can capture His heart. Remember that God is not hiding so that He *can't* be found. He is very careful to hide so that He *can* be found. He *wants* you to find Him. The day Isaiah found Him, somehow, in some way, the conditions were just right and the eternal patterns of His presence suddenly appeared in front of Isaiah.

Look at the first few words of the verse that begins: "In the year that King Uzziah died . . ." Death and dependence began to show up in Isaiah's life. God cannot be King in your life until all other kings are gone. If you've been depending on the king of the fleshly realm, then the patterns of God's presence are never going to appear.

Isaiah served under a popular king who committed the same basic sin that King Saul committed in the beginning of the kingdom.[10] Uzziah's chief sin, and the cause of his unclean flesh, was that he mishandled in presumption the glory of God. He transgressed in his presumptuous approach to God, doing it *his* way instead of God's way. He knew better; he just chose to do things his own way.

He sought God in the days of Zechariah, who had understanding in the visions of God; and *as long as he sought the* LORD, *God made him prosper . . .* *But when he was strong his heart was lifted up, to his destruction, for he transgressed against the* LORD *his God by entering the temple of the* LORD *to burn incense on the altar of incense.* So Azariah the priest went in after him, and with him were eighty priests of the LORD—valiant men. And they withstood King Uzziah, and said to him, "It is not for you, Uzziah, to burn incense to the LORD, but for the priests, the sons of Aaron, who are consecrated to burn incense. Get out of the sanctuary, for you have trespassed! You shall have no honor from the LORD God." Then Uzziah became furious; and he had a censer in his hand to burn incense. And while he was angry with the priests, leprosy broke out on his forehead . . . King Uzziah was a leper until the day of his death. *He dwelt in an isolated house,* because he was a leper; for *he was cut off from the house of the* LORD. Then Jotham his son was over the king's house, judging the people of the land.[11]

Where David offered brokenness and totally dependent love to God and was invited into God's inner chambers of intimacy, Uzziah assumed he was worthy and barged into God's chambers with an offering immersed in the fragrance of pride, arrogance, and presumption.

KING UZZIAH SUCCUMBED TO THE SEDUCTION OF STRENGTH

This godly king began well, but *he succumbed to the seduction of strength*. God spared Uzziah's life. (That is more than what Uzzah received when he presumed to underestimate and undervalue God's holiness in David's day. Ironically Uzzah's name means "strength."[12])

In a way, Uzziah was just a dressed-up Uzzah trying to touch the same thing that the pauper was killed for. If we don't make the church "Uzzah-friendly," we tend to make it "Uzziah-friendly" so we can welcome the king of the flesh. King Uzziah hadn't even left the temple before God permanently branded him with leprosy on his forehead, a physical ailment called by the same name as our spiritual ailment—he was *unclean*.

Uzziah's prideful flesh came into unauthorized and unprotected contact with the holiness of God, and when confronted with his sin, he dared to rise up in rebellion and defiance against the priests of God. His unclean nature rose to the surface, permanently revealing what he really was. It disqualified him to rule, and his son came in as regent while he probably continued to rule as the power behind the throne. In the beginning, Uzziah prospered, but when he stopped seeking, he also stopped prospering.

He also was disqualified from being buried with the kings of Judah because of his leprosy. It seems Isaiah was still mourning the fall of this anointed but tragically condemned leader when God *restructured* his understanding of the holy.

Perhaps the church suffers from the Uzziah Syndrome today. We insist on approaching God our way, and we say that everything is fine. Our way will be the acceptable way because we are sure we know what God likes. We think we can continue to "feed Him" like a trained pet on a chain with our crafted sermons, serial liturgies, and orchestrated prostrations in religious pride and arrogance.

God is about to brand many of us with an outward leprosy that marks us as "cut off from the house of God," or what Paul said was "having a form of godliness but denying [and lacking] its power."[13] The apostle went on to urge that we "turn away" from such people. Has God turned away from us because of our empty religious forms? Has our presumption polluted our offerings and disqualified us from residence in His presence?

The only cure for the Uzziah Syndrome is an Isaiah experience with God that you will never get over. Most of us never make it to that point because we get angry when we are confronted with the truth. We get angry instead of yielding to sorrowful repentance, and we insist on swinging our sacred religious censers filled with unauthorized and unacceptable offerings. What we need are burning lips and a hot heart. One coal from His altar will cure our arrogance.

What we should really pray for is this: "Show me Your glory, Lord. You told us to seek Your face, and now we're trotting around in the diapers of immaturity. We don't even know what we are doing. We just know Daddy is in the house, and we're hunting for You."

There is room for only one king in the economy of God. I recently noticed that when King Herod rejected the baby Jesus, the infant King of kings evacuated to Egypt and did not return until Herod was dead.

If you insist on retaining the rulership over your life, God will just evacuate and wait until something dies and dependency is re-created.

> What we need are burning lips and a hot heart. One coal from His altar will cure our arrogance.

Then He comes right back. The Scriptures say, "Now when Herod was dead," Jesus and His family returned to Israel.[14] *Dead fleshly kings make way for living spiritual kings and kingdoms.* That is the divine pattern. "When Uzziah died . . ."

Isaiah was the king's cousin, and he had the inside track; he was the "king's preacher." All of a sudden, the king died, and it wasn't clear who would take care of Isaiah. His dependency appeared, and the pattern started to appear to create the climate for a visitation. Frost began to be etched on the window, and he said, "I saw the Lord . . ."

How many times had he been to the temple *before* this occasion and *thought* he saw the Lord? You see, we really don't have measuring sticks of His presence. It's difficult. I travel frequently and participate in a lot of incredible services. Sometimes people will say, "You'll have to stay, and we'll have to keep having these services. We've never really experienced anything like this."

I'll be really honest; I would never offend them, but I will tell you this: By the measure of the encounters that I have heard of, we are not at that place where it's time for some protracted meetings. I am not against protracted services; I spent three years returning weekly to Baltimore for protracted meetings at the Lord's leading. Sometimes the level of God rises knee-deep, and that is the greatest level some people have ever experienced. If it fills up a little bit more, perhaps waist-high, they'll say, "Oh, we'll build three tabernacles and stay here."[15]

I'm grateful for every rise in the spiritual water level, but "deep calls unto deep."

Even if you have personally experienced it at levels that are neck-high, remain grateful for every rise and fall of the water, but just keep saying, "There's more . . . there are waters to swim in."[16]

Only three times in my life have I been in places where I said, "*This* is what I'm talking about . . ." I long for more of those moments. I'm grateful for every rise in the spiritual water level, but "deep calls unto deep."[17] My "deep" hunger cries for His "deep" water. I feel like echoing the cry of Moses: "Please, show me Your glory!"[18]

Now, how many times had Isaiah "been to church" and left "high-fiving" everybody, saying, "Whoo, man, that was awesome, incredible! We had church!" because he didn't have a "ruler" to gauge that by?

Until one day God really did show up. The conditions were just right for the pattern of His presence to appear, and "suddenly" Isaiah saw the Lord high and lifted up.

Read the first five chapters of the book of Isaiah, and notice their context and content. They say, "Woe is me . . . woe is you . . . and woe is everybody."

Then he had the God encounter noted in Isaiah 6.

After that, there are sixty more chapters of incredible prophetic declarations. Not "woe is me and woe is you," but He was "high and lifted up" and "unto us a Son is given" and "the government will be upon His shoulder" and "Wonderful, Counselor, Mighty God, Everlasting Father."[19]

What's the difference? *If you ever see Him, it changes everything.* Suddenly you are aware of something. Even if the frost is not on the windowpane, you are aware of the potential for it to be there, and you just keep trying to adjust the temperature for that appearing.

So do you "chase" God? Yes. Do you "catch" God? You capture His heart, and He manifests His presence.

You're outside with a skinned knee and your desperate cries pull God into your dimension.

As I wrote in *God's Favorite House:*

The six-winged seraphim were simply doing what they were created to do. They were crying out the praises of God in perfection and beating the atmosphere with their wings while covering their faces and their feet in humility. Then everything stops when God Almighty hears the pitiful refrain rising faintly from the chaos of the earth below: "He is holy, He is holy. . . ." He quickly commands the angelic hosts, "Be quiet." (I can almost hear the angels in the rear whisper to one another, *"There He goes again."*)

. . . Meanwhile, the angelic hosts who once heard Lucifer the archangel rattle the heavens with thunderous worship and breathtaking celestial music are saying, *"What is man that You are mindful of him, and the son of man that You visit him?"*[20]

Oblivious to every whispered question, God hushes the angels and says to Michael and Gabriel,

"Look, guys, I'm going to have to leave it with you."

"Why? What is it, Lord?"

"Well, you see, I heard something that I just can't ignore. I heard the song of the redeemed again . . ."

In the twinkling of an eye, the manifest presence of God is transported from Heaven to the middle of a tear-stained circle singing, "Holy, holy, holy is the Lord . . ." *God leaves His magnificent throne of Heaven and comes to earth to be enthroned on the pitiful praises of His people.*[21]

If you ever have an encounter with the manifest presence of God, it will ruin church for you. From then on, you put up with church. What you really want is, "Come on, God."

Man-centered sermons and songs will make you sick. Going through the motions will just drive you nuts. "What are you trying to do?" People can't even see what you're looking at. They think you're looking out the window, but you are looking for the pattern to appear on the windowpane. You're not even looking at the same things.

Your heavenly Father wants you to rediscover the joy of innocence and excitement at His presence. When we grow up to the arrogance of adolescence, we can't capture His heart because we think, *Oh, it's just You. Oh, it's just church; they're just singing another song. It's just another sermon.*

The process is not hiding; the process is finding and the joy of discovery. Behind every song could be the fresh discovery of His presence. When passionate pleas replace dry discourses, "church" can become the celebration of His presence it was always meant to be. He was always there waiting, but the conditions were not correct.

For frost to appear, not only do the conditions have to be right outside the window, but the temperature has to be just right inside as well. It appears where those two meet. When brokenness appears in our lives, openness appears in the heavens.

Perhaps Isaiah had an encounter at the temple that day because he had just come back from a funeral. He was hurting a bit more than normal. Suddenly his earthly dependence had been cut off and perhaps he felt he had to pursue a heavenly dependence on the presence of God.

God will take advantage of your desperate feelings to create a dependency on Him. Thirty seconds in the manifest presence of God can change everything. It can change a nation, it can change your destiny, and it can rearrange your future. You'll never be the same.

Isaiah lived in an age of religious apostasy. Things had gone awry religiously. Some people enjoy pointing out all the things that are wrong with the church. I have news for them: we can twist all the dials and pull all the levers that we want to on earth, but we are never going to fix it. If you really want to fix it, you fix it in the heavenlies. You can have an encounter with Him right in the middle of religious apostasy. Your desperation causes you to look past the circumstances, past the veil.

> When passionate pleas replace dry discourses, "church" can become the celebration of His presence it was always meant to be.

LOOK PAST THE PRIESTS AND THROUGH THE SMOKE

Isaiah had been in the temple many times, but probably what he saw most of the time was the smoke from the priests. Finally he looked past the smoke. At some point in your discovery of the presence of God, you have to look *past the priests and through the smoke*. If you are singing only because a song leader is singing, then you've stopped at the veil. But if suddenly you step out of this dimension and step into that one, you are not just worshiping because someone is leading; you begin worshiping because *He* is there.

There's a validation that comes with the presence of God that changes your perspective. Isaiah had an encounter. He stumbled into God's presence!

He saw the glory of God *and His train* filled the temple. According to Colossians, God disarmed and "made a public spectacle" of Satan and his principalities and powers.[22] In ancient times, a victorious general would put his foot on the neck of the conquered king in the city square, and he would cut off his enemy's royal robes and strip off his jewels. Then the general would bring back the captured royal remnants so they could be sewn into the royal robes *of his own king*. The loser's jewels would be displayed on the walls of the conqueror's city. You could tell how many victories an emperor had won by the number of "additions" that had been placed on the train of his robe.

When Isaiah saw the Lord, he said, "His train filled the temple." How many victories has He won? You think you've had an encounter with the glory of God? Wait until you've glimpsed Him in His glory!

If you read Ezekiel's description of Lucifer, you will see a list of nine precious stones that covered the original angelic form of the anointed cherub who fell in his pride and presumption.[23] A very similar collection of stones shows up in the book of Revelation—included in a list of twelve stones publicly displayed in foundations of the walls of New Jerusalem, the city of the King of kings.[24]

My point is, you think you've seen God? Ask Isaiah how many times he went to "church" before the one day he really saw Him.

Never Underestimate the Potential of One Service

If in infantile immaturity, you ever throw back the door and suddenly see Him, exclaiming, "There He is—Daddy!" then all you will ever want to do the rest of your life is to discover His presence. That is it. You will just want to be with Him. Never underestimate the potential of one service.

Does God hide? Yes. That's the easy answer. But He doesn't hide so that He can't be found. He's very, very careful to hide so that He can be found. In His infiniteness, He could hide where you could never find Him, but He hides in the folds of time so that while you're singing a little song, praying a prayer, you discover Him. He didn't hide far away; He hid close. You can find Him in worship. Your passion is how you discover Him. Passion—not perfection—pulls God from His dimension into yours.

He will take your imperfect praise and perfect it in His ears. He does it in the same way that a mother "perfects" the imperfect childish attempts of her baby to express her desires in words for the first time.

God says, "It's not how pretty they do it. It's just that they are My off-spring." *He would rather hear you stumble through a song with a voice like a cracked foghorn than to hear the six-winged seraphim surround Him with chants of "holy" in tones of heavenly perfection.*[25]

How do you get the conditions right to find Him?

1. You can pursue Him like a toddler. If you find His feet, you find His face.

2. At other times, desperation pulls Him from His dimension into yours. *He finds you!*

There really is no formula. We have allowed the structure of man to impede the passion of a child. That's why the Master Teacher said, "Assuredly, I say to you, unless you are converted *and become as little children,* you will by no means enter the kingdom of heaven."[26]

We need to set everything aside at times and say, "God, I can't catch You and I can't figure You out either; but I sure do need You."

My youngest daughter often can't get me outside of the house in her wholeness, but when she displays her brokenness, I'm there. As long as you are pretending everything is okay, He will allow you to go through it on your own. What He really wants to create is an air of dependency on Him. Quit trying to display your independence; start displaying your dependence and see what happens. I am desperately dependent on Him.

"Isaiah, what happened?"

"I don't know. After all the things I'd counted on just died, and after the burial, I went to the church and I just cried out. That's when He showed up."

"Isaiah, hasn't He always been there?"

"Yes, He was always there, but the conditions were not right for Him to display Himself. I caught a glimpse of Him that day."

Maybe that's what it means when you are a God Catcher: "I caught a glimpse, I saw Him, and His train filled the temple. I've never been the same since He touched my lips."[27]

It's not just your words; it is your passion for His presence. How hungry are you? How desperate are you?

You're pulling God into your dimension . . . you're catching Him. You found His feet; now you can have a face-to-face encounter.

God hides in the same places again and again . . . nothing fancy; it's the same stuff. However, you cannot *formulize* love. If you attempt to use formulas and equations, God will move the door to those places every time. In this way, the secret place is a secret every time.

Passion knows no logic. Logic would have said to Mary of the alabaster box, "Don't do this. You can't afford it." But passion said, "I can't afford *not* to." What did that cause? She discovered Him. The disciples thought they had Jesus in the room that day, but they had Him in one dimension. She opened the door to a whole other dimension. The temperature gradient was just right, and He displayed His glory.

God wants to display His glory to you; He's simply waiting for you to get the conditions just right. The temperature of your heart has to be set on "Desperation." Then the "frost of His presence" will begin to appear on the windowpanes where God comes into your life.

Perhaps Isaiah spent only thirty seconds in the presence of the King, high and lifted up; in any case, it totally transformed his life and ministry. Called "the Messianic prophet" of the Old Testament, Isaiah is quoted in the New Testament more than any other prophet.[28] After his God-encounter, Isaiah's theme changed. He no longer prophesied of a thing he *hoped* might come to pass, or of something he *imagined* looked a certain way. Isaiah "saw His glory and spoke of Him," according to John.[29]

He had seen and heard for himself. His lips had been cleansed and anointed by the burning coal of God's glory. He could now speak of His glory! In just a moment of time, Isaiah became the prophet of His presence more than of His "presents."

The single most important God encounter in your life may well occur on the day you return from a funeral. Perhaps the death of your dreams or the death of your ministry will usher you into His presence before He "hides real good." It may be your dying to self or to ambition that causes

> Passion knows no logic. Logic would have said to Mary of the alabaster box, "Don't do this. You can't afford it." But passion said, "I can't afford not to."

you to encounter Him by surprise on the hundredth time you enter the doors of that little church on the back side of nowhere.

Like Moses, we've seen a lot of things, but we really want one thing more than any other: "Show us Your glory, Lord. We seek Your face in our immaturity. We don't really know how to do it, but we know You are here. We are desperately hunting for You."

It is time to allow the king of all other pursuits to die. Let the pursuit of His presence become your single magnificent obsession.

Break our hearts, Lord God. Set us on fire with incredible hunger until nothing else and nothing less than Your presence will satisfy.

3

I Don't Know Whether to Laugh or Cry

CAUGHT IN THE MIDDLE OF WHAT IS AND WHAT CAN BE

SOMETIMES I THINK THAT SATISFACTION MAY BE THE greatest enemy of the purposes of God in the church and in the world. Far too many God Chasers stop the chase to celebrate their best pace in the last race. We forget to resume the pursuit when we stop to build monuments to a momentary visitation of God's presence.

When we turn our focus from His face to the *memory* of His appearance yesterday, we may find that He has moved on to greater exploits *outside* our limited vision and perception of divine purpose. Jesus commanded us to take up our cross and follow Him *daily*—not as it fits in our schedule.[1]

The only way to regain our spiritual balance is to stop pretending that everything is all right. It isn't. How many times do we go to meetings and say, "Oh, this is great"? I don't mean to be ungrateful in any way, but if those meetings aren't leading to the salvation of the city, then they fall short of the potential resident in God's glory. We are too quick to become artificially satisfied after we race to false finish lines.

One of Satan's greatest tricks is to make us feel satisfied as if we have arrived somewhere. The truth is that we can "fall into the ditch" on either side of the narrow road. We can fail to be grateful for the many visitations and blessings of God and see the river of His presence run dry quickly. God refuses to honor those who do not acknowledge and honor Him.

On the other hand, we can do what many in the church have done: we can major on being grateful and lose the ragged edge of spiritual hunger that put us in the race in the first place. It is hunger that *keeps* us in the pursuit.

We tend to satisfy our hunger pains through the performance of minor religious duties such as once-a-week church attendance or an occasional prayer on the run. Hunger has ceased to be part of our religious vocabulary because it is considered "undignified" by today's spiritual elite. They don't realize that hunger is among the most attractive things they have to offer to their Creator.

Lovers are attracted by their beloved's passion, not by casual or disinterested mental assent to their respective "attractiveness." Our divine Bridegroom is no different. That is why I say it is entirely possible to be grateful and desperate at the same time. *I am very grateful for what He has done, but I am also very desperate for what He can do.*

The book of Ezra contains an unusual account of the day the Jewish remnant dedicated the rebuilt foundations of the fallen temple in Jerusalem:

> Then all the people shouted with a great shout, when they praised the LORD, because the foundation of the house of the LORD was laid. But many of the priests and Levites and heads of the fathers' houses, *old men who had seen the first temple, wept with a loud voice* when the foundation of this temple was laid before their eyes. Yet many shouted aloud for joy, so that the people *could not discern the noise of the shout of joy from the noise of the weeping* of the people, for the people shouted with a loud shout, and the sound was heard afar off.[2]

> Hunger has ceased to be part of our religious vocabulary because it is considered "undignified" by today's spiritual elite.

The younger men had never seen the great temple of Solomon built before Jerusalem was overrun by Babylon. They were the children of the captivity who had never seen "revival." So they got all excited and began to lift their voices and rejoice, "Oh, this is it! God is here, and it is glorious!"

The older men who were there began to weep when they saw the dimensions of the rebuilt temple foundations. The cacophony of passion was so loud and intermingled that the Scriptures say it was impossible to distinguish the noise of the weeping from the noise of the rejoicing.

What was the difference between the two groups of men? The older men were personally acquainted with the events of history. They had seen what God had done in the past when Jerusalem and Israel were in their finest hour. They rejoiced to see the foundations of God's house laid again, but they also wept because it couldn't begin to compare to what it once was.

I think I know what happened. When those elderly priests, Levites, and family patriarchs saw the rebuilt foundations of the temple in the generation of captivity, they said, "No, we will not be satisfied!" It is as if they proverbially "held God's feet to the fire" and said, "You promised us that the glory of the latter house is supposed to be greater than the former house, God. We are holding You to Your fullest potential."[3]

> This odd mix of joy with sorrow, of satisfaction with hunger, is common wherever God shows up.

At some point, you need to decide and declare, "Lord, I thank You for what You've done, but I am desperate for what You can do. I thank You for rebuilding the ruins of the past, and I thank You for what You've done in my church and my city. But You are not the God of limitation and lack. I'm desperate for what I know You *can* do! Open the heavens over this city. Open the heavens over the churches, schools, and families in this place."

That kind of desperation and brokenness can pull God from His hiding place. No wonder He said, "Seek My face." God is just waiting to reveal His face to somebody who is desperate enough and bold enough to pull Him out of hiding.

It is entirely possible and even *desirable* for you

to be grateful and desperate at the same time. It is expressed in terms like these: "We're not ungrateful for what You've already done, God, but we're desperate for what You *can* do. We thank You for Your touch, Lord. The only thing we're frustrated about is that we *know* there had to be more of You."

This is the way the older priests felt when they saw the rebuilt temple foundation dedicated. Ezra said the noise of the weepers and the noise of the rejoicers could not be distinguished from each other. I propose that this is the proper posture for the church. *We are grateful for what He has done, but we are also desperate for what He can do.* This odd mix of joy with sorrow, of satisfaction with hunger, is common wherever God shows up.

Amos spoke of a time "when the plowman shall overtake the reaper, and the treader of grapes him who sows seed; the mountains shall drip with sweet wine."[4]

What am I saying? When I hear God's people get excited and say, "Isn't this great? A new church is being built, and there is unbelievable unity in the city!" I think of the things I've seen and the decades-old yearning in my heart, and then I struggle to tell them through my tears, "Yes, it *is* great; but there *has to be more.* You haven't seen anything yet."

"What are you talking about, Tommy? Are you saying there will be a better service than this?"

People ask me these things all the time, and I wonder if we are even on the same page. Perhaps there will be more powerful services when there are more passionate servants. I've really never known of a dry *service*—just dry *servants!* And I am talking about more than *our* hunger. It plays an important part, but it is His hunger responding to ours that causes Him to move His throne and set it up right here in the midst of our praises.

YIELD TO THE HUNGER FOR HIM

We should be reassured and encouraged when God brings us to the point where we don't know whether to laugh or cry. If nothing else, it means that

God is at work in you "both to will and to do for His good pleasure."[5] A holy hunger is being fired up inside you that will take you to the edge of dissatisfaction and joy at the same time. When you yield to the hunger, you really won't care what you say anymore. You will say, "If I can just touch the hem of His garment . . . If I can have an encounter with Him." Once you reach the point where it is all you can do to maintain your composure, my question is, Why try? When you don't know whether to laugh or cry, you may be in a good place.

Is it possible for fullness and emptiness to exist side by side? Yes.

Can deep satisfaction and endless hunger coexist in one heart? Yes.

How can joy and aching longing radiate from the same face at the same time? Ask Ezra, the Old Testament priest. He knew the answer. So did David the psalmist and Paul the apostle. They lived constantly in this strange state of heavenly tension between consuming desire and overwhelming satisfaction in His presence.

> We need Him every moment of every day. To say anything else is ludicrous.

I promise you that true revival cannot take place in the absence of either component. We must be grateful for all the things God has done for us (He will not reward ungratefulness in human hearts), and we must be continually desperate for more of His manifest presence. He is strangely attracted to our desperation and "holy appetite" for His visitation and manifest presence. It all goes back to the heart.

On the day you repented of your sins and received Jesus Christ as Lord and Savior, did you walk away thinking that you had "enough" of God to do you for a lifetime? It has been said before, but I'll say it again: that is like saying that one meal will supply all your body's needs for the rest of your life. It won't. The day of your salvation was just that, the beginning of a new life under a "new Son."

You need constant exposure to His Word, His Spirit, and His people, the church. His presence is literally the air your spirit-man breathes. Jesus wasn't talking just for the fun of it when He called Himself the Bread of Life. He is our food, our water, our joy, our Rock and Shield, our Healer, our Deliverer, our Redeemer, our Shepherd, our Great High Priest, our Advocate. Need I say more? We need Him every moment of every day. To say anything else is ludicrous.

Jesus said, "Without Me you can do nothing."[6] What does *that* mean? The branches of a vine are "grateful" to belong to the vine and the root of the vine. But they also have an ongoing desperate need to draw more and more sustenance from that nurturing vine each day. This is the Lord's natural picture of being grateful and desperate at the same time.

Since we have no record of God doing anything by accident or in ignorance, why should we assume that Jesus accidentally used what scholars call the "present imperative" voice when He said this about prayer:

> So I say to you, Ask *and* keep on asking and it shall be given you; seek *and* keep on seeking and you shall find; knock *and* keep on knocking and the door shall be opened to you.[7]

It sure seems to me that Jesus was telling us to remain in a perpetual state of asking, seeking, and knocking. What I don't see in the New Testament is any command requiring us (or even *permitting us*) to be complacent, apathetic, or lethargic.

Even the "Greatest Worshiper" Left His Presence Hungry

King David was perhaps the greatest earthly praise and worship leader of all time. He set the standards of worship that we are still trying to match today, and he did it before the Cross and the advent of the Holy Spirit. Yet the same man who used to sit in God's presence in the open-air "tabernacle of David" told the Lord:

> As the deer pants for the water brooks,
> So pants my soul for You, O God.
> My soul thirsts for God, for the living God.
> When shall I come and appear before God?[8]

Jacob, the Old Testament patriarch, had a checkered past like that of many of us today. When God began to work with him, he became a desperate man. He was grateful for the vision of heaven's staircase and the continuation of God's promises to his father, but he wanted more.

He was so desperate for a miracle and a second chance that he wrestled all through the night with a man who was most likely the preincarnate Christ.[9] Jacob refused to release him until he'd received a blessing. He was frantic for a fresh start and a new name, so the Lord renamed him Israel and blessed him. He also gave him a permanent wound in the hip to remind him of his neediness before God.[10]

Simeon was an elderly prayer warrior in an age of apostasy who prayed constantly in the temple at Jerusalem. He took comfort in the promises of God, but he wanted *more*. He received a promise from God that he would literally see the Messiah of Israel before he died.

The long years kept going by until the day came when he finally saw young Jesus in the temple. In that moment, the prophetic dam broke in Simeon's heart and he prophesied over Jesus, uttering perhaps the first words of prophecy heard in

> All John knew was that if the Master was within touching distance, then he would go straight for the heart.

Israel since the passing of the prophets four hundred years earlier. He openly expressed his gratefulness for God's promises, but it was his hunger for more that kept him alive long enough to see and prophesy over the Messiah.[11]

John the disciple was grateful for the Lord's companionship, but his desperate hunger to be closer to Jesus caused him to lay his head on the Lord's chest at every opportunity. We can safely assume that John didn't care if the other disciples talked about him, belittled him, or expressed their jealousy over his shameless search for more of the Lord's love. All he knew was that if the Master was within touching distance, then he would go straight for the heart.

John's "God addiction" isn't something to be scorned; it is something to be sought after and duplicated in our own lives. John's addiction for God's presence continued all of his life, long after Jesus had ascended to the Father and long after the excitement of the early days had faded away.

In the end, John outlasted everyone else in the inner circle of disciples. It was this man, the one who spent the most time closest to the heart of the Messiah, who received the final "Revelation of Jesus Christ."

CHASING GOD IN THE SPIRIT ON THE ISLE OF PATMOS

By the end of the book, we find John *still* spending every spare moment positioning himself near to the heart of God. Perhaps that is why God chose him over all the other more visible and charismatic leaders of the early church. John was chasing God in the Spirit when God turned and "caught him" on the Isle of Patmos.

He was literally *caught up* into the heavenly scene. He caught God, and God caught him. There is a holy lift in His presence. "Lord, lift us up where we belong, where the eagles fly." Passionate pursuit has the potential to change your perspective, like a father lifting up his child to give the child a better view. John was lifted above time to get a better view of eternity.

I was in the Spirit on the Lord's Day, and I heard behind me a loud voice, as of a trumpet, saying, "I am the Alpha and the Omega, the First and the Last," and, "What you see, write in a book and send it to the seven churches."[12]

John, like Moses before him, wanted to see the face of his beloved Master once again. In the process, he received a whole lot more. When John said he was "in the Spirit on the Lord's Day," he was in the process of "creating urgency" in the spirit realm. When you pray with persistence, worship with abandon, or fast in hunger and desperation, you create heavenly urgency and passion that are virtually irresistible to your Maker and heavenly Father. Too many of us miss the mark of passion when we seek the arrival of revival instead of the face of the Reviver.

> Too many of us miss the mark of passion when we seek the arrival of revival instead of the face of the Reviver.

Of all the disciples who were in the room when Mary dared to interrupt man's agenda to anoint the Master with oil from her alabaster box, John alone may have understood the value of her sacrifice.[13] Why? He understood the superior power of passion over the protocol of logic and intellect. Logic and intellect have their proper place, but it is not in the intimacy of the Holy of Holies.

How many of us have given our children or our spouses a gift that we really couldn't afford? Intimacy overrode intellect; passion overcame logic. That's the power of positioning versus the power of petitioning. If you are in the position of a face-seeker,[14] your position has urgency.

While the other disciples peppered Jesus with questions of theology to feed the mind, John watched Mary feed the heart of God with her tears of worship and broken offering of sacrificial oil. Perhaps he, too, shed some tears on the chest of his beloved Master over such an open display of hunger and brokenness.

We must seek Him while He may be found. It doesn't matter whether we begin at His feet with eyes filled with the tears of brokenhearted passion or we move straight to His heart with our whole being in complete surrender and desperation. He responds to the cries of the hungry, but He can't do anything with the complacent requests and halfhearted queries of the satisfied and self-sufficient.

LEANING ON THE EVERLASTING "CRUTCH" OF GLORY

It has been claimed by our atheist critics that Christianity is nothing but a crutch for the disabled and weak people of the world. They have no idea!

> *Lord, I openly confess my poverty of spirit. Like the boast of Paul the apostle, my only boast is of my absolute dependence upon You.[15] I am permanently, incurably, profoundly, and desperately God-challenged and weak without You! I can't live, function, or produce apart from You. I'm humanly handicapped!*

I think we've become too familiar with the pleasure of His provisions and the blessings of His hand. We've forsaken the tears of repentance and passionate desperation known by the revered saints of the past. It is time to rediscover the power of passionate and fervent prayer. It allows us to tap the resurrection force resident in the act of repentance; it can express our all-consuming hunger for a fresh encounter with the God of eternity.

Yes, it is entirely possible to be desperately grateful and desperately hungry at the same time. There are a lot of people who are happier with church than I am, but I must confess that I'm weary with it all. I am tired of endless church meetings and the constant buzz of man's activity in the name of God. I'm desperate for Him. He is the One I fell in love with—all the other things just get in the way of my pursuit of Him. It is Him that I want; it is Him that I'm hungry for.

> "Jacob, how did you pull God from His hiding place? What compelled Him to open a window in the heavens and extend a ladder to your stone pillow and hard-place bedside?"
>
> "I just got desperate and broken. I didn't even realize how close I was to Him."

If you find yourself feeling both grateful for His momentary visitation and desperately hungry for more, then I must say that you have no idea how close you are to an encounter with Him that will change your life. Are you desperate to learn how Moses won God's promise to show him more of His glory? Are you hungry to discover how Jacob prevailed in his wrestling match with divinity and received a new name?

What pulled God from His hidden place behind the wings of the seraphim to say to Moses, "Okay, I'll show you My glory—but only from the back side"?[16] Was it because Moses said, "Now look, God, You should show me Your glory because we've got everything planned out. We have all our proverbial ducks in a row, and everything is organized and set up"?

No, none of us can build a church building that is pretty enough to attract God. No congregation can accumulate enough stained glass, construct a steeple tall enough, present music that is beautiful enough, or provide enough good preaching to pull Him from His throne in heaven.

If those things would work, then God would have rebuilt Solomon's grand temple in Jerusalem. Nothing in ancient or modern architecture could begin to compare with that magnificent edifice, but God showed no interest in rebuilding it.

God Confounds the Wise and Disturbs the Religious Performers

Instead, He confounded the wise and disturbed the religious performers by choosing David's lowly tabernacle built on Zion without walls, veil, or the elaborate finery of man's hands found in Moses' tabernacle and Solomon's temple:

> After this I will return
> And will rebuild the tabernacle of David, which has fallen down;
> I will rebuild its ruins,
> And I will set it up;
> So that the rest of mankind may seek the LORD.[17]

When God said these words, He made it clear that His chief interest is in your desperation, hunger, and passion for His presence. *He is not after performance; He wants passion.*

Remember that when passion reenters the church, His presence comes back through the door as well. We may not like it; it may offend our egos and bruise our theology, but that is just the way it is. Pray this prayer with me if you are in the place of coexistent gratefulness and desperation:

Lord, let us leave Your presence more hungry than when we came in. May we always be grateful but desperate; thankful but still hungry. May our first and last prayer to You eternally be, "I'm hungry for You!"

4

SHALL WE GATHER AT THE RIVER OR JUST JUMP IN?

THE PERILS OF VALUING PROGRAM ABOVE PRESENCE

I REMEMBER AS A LITTLE BOY WONDERING ABOUT THE words of some of the great hymns they used to sing in church. I just didn't have a clue about some of them. I remember listening to the adults sing, "Angels *peck* on me from heaven's open door . . ." Older and wiser now, I know the proper phrase was, "Angels beckon me," but back then, in my immature logic, I thought to myself, *Well, if they have wings, maybe they have beaks too.*

When the older folks sang, "Shall we gather at the river," I had no clue about the spiritual applications of the word *river*. All I could think of were the times I fished on the river with my grandfather. I didn't see any use in "gathering" at the river if I couldn't float on it, fish in it, cross it, or jump in for a refreshing swim. I never really understood the songs we used to sing until I met the One we were singing about. I wonder how long, in our collective immaturity, we have sung about His presence without ever diving in?

I'm not making fun of the cherished hymns—at times, they can move me into His presence as nothing else can. Yet the fact is that *rivers are to cross and transition through.* The Israelites in the wilderness chose to embrace all the negative reports and the "safe" counsel of men instead of the "riskier" counsel of God. As a result, an entire generation died homeless. They never stepped into the water of transition from the deliverance of bondage to the possession of God's promise. It's time for this generation to dive into the river.

Many churches appear to believe that God is going to come because they have a nice building or the prettiest stained glass in town, or because their choir sings well and the preacher preaches well. There is nothing wrong with stained glass or well-trained choirs, and preaching is obviously a thoroughly biblical foundation of the Christian life. However, I don't mean to burst a cherished bubble, but God isn't impressed with any of these things. *They are for us,* not Him. He comes to our meetings only in response to our worship and our hunger. Remember that earthly brokenness creates heavenly openness. For that reason, I am compelled by the Spirit of God to make what may be one of the oddest statements you will ever see in a Christian book:

Don't let church obscure your view of God.

My middle daughter was only four when we drove to an overlook at the Grand Canyon and stepped out of the car to see the wonders of that place. She wanted to know what it was, so we told her, "It is a big hole in the ground in America with a lot of big, pretty rocks."

Religion causes us to gather together for all the wrong reasons.

We stopped long enough in the gravel parking lot to point to the colorful walls of the canyon in the distance and say excitedly, "Look at the rocks, baby!" Then we began to walk to the overlook site. She kept saying, "Look at the rocks!" so we assumed she was following us in wide-eyed wonder. When we looked back, we noticed that she wasn't looking at the Grand Canyon at all. She had picked up a handful of gravel from the parking lot. She carefully cradled those rocks and carried them with great reverence as she said, "Look—American rocks!"

That is a picture of the church. The Holy

Spirit is pointing to the coming of the Father in all His glory, and we are still scrabbling in the parking lot, digging for religious paving stones to say, "Look . . ." Religion causes us to gather together for all the wrong reasons.

We gather to throw stones at people who are different or people who don't measure up to our own individual brand of religious righteousness (man's works). In some cases, we even pick up some rocks to pelt people who dare to be "more spiritual" than we are. Sinners hear countless stories on the news and in the local barber and beauty shops about Christian people who gather to debate the commands of God and come to verbal blows over meaningless jots and tittles while shoving aside the most important things.

We also gather together to proudly display our accomplishments and works to God, not realizing that we are asking Him to bless and honor our personal pile of filthy rags. We lift up our tithes and offerings of gold to Him as if He needed them. Like my little daughter cradling those worthless rocks in the parking lot of the Grand Canyon, we carefully cradle our gold and reluctantly place it at His feet as if it were of inestimable value. Yet we are merely offering God "paving rocks" from His golden streets instead of placing our focus on His face—the true source of all wonder and wealth in the kingdom.[1]

God has to break through our programs before He can break out and manifest His presence among us. He has to demolish our artificial intelligence (our dim and sometimes haughty imitation of His omniscience) and artificial spirituality (our programs) to bring in the real thing and take a city or nation.

Unfortunately it is a rare church that can handle the divine call to self-demolition and reignition by the fire of God. Essentially it means we must invite the cleansing fire of God into our meetings. We forget that not much is left over once the divine fire comes to examine our lives. Everything that is rooted in man's foundation is consumed; only the things of God remain. That means we have to face a "garden of Gethsemane" experience *before* we can see His face.

HOW DO GOD CHASERS CORNER HIM?

The more I pursue this subject, the more I perceive its simplicity. *We want equations and formulas, the stuff and structure of man's programs.* Even at our best, when somehow we align our hearts with the heart of God and He visits us for a moment, we instinctively grope for a formula to re-create it. The desire for more is godly, but the methodology is not. When Satan seduced Eve into eating the fruit of the Tree of the Knowledge of Good and Evil in the garden, he was merely offering Eve an artificial and illegal means to become like God—something God intended for her all along. The desire wasn't necessarily evil, but the methodology brought death.

If you have a good service, and the choir sings the right song, the next thing you know somebody will say, "Hey, sing that song again! We want to go back to that same place again. If the formula worked once, it will work again." No, it won't. God will move the door to the secret place and change the point of access so that His relationship with you doesn't become an empty ritual commemorating what once was. He wants to preserve the joy and freshness of our encounters together, and equations and formulas do exactly the opposite.

> We must have an uncontainable hunger to entertain our uncontainable God. That automatically disqualifies the religious program.

I try to be nice when I visit church congregations around the world, but at times a spirit of spiritual violence or righteous indignation rises up in me and I say, "You're close, but stop trying to keep God in your box." It appears that God sends His glory and presence to us in waves for reasons known only to Him. Another wave of God's presence is about to hit the shore of the church and the nations. It has happened before in

differing times and seasons. I've carefully studied the history of revival in America and around the world, but another wave is coming that is going to be different—if we cooperate.

God wants to "break outside of the box." That means that our hunger has to get bigger than the religious box we've built over multiplied centuries of man-centered religious practice. We must have an *uncontainable hunger* to entertain our *uncontainable God*. That automatically disqualifies the religious program. By definition, a program is a prepackaged, manageable, predictable reproduction of what worked once for somebody somewhere. But God doesn't do "out of the box revival."

Revival comes when the Father shows up and man shows up at the same time and same place and a supernatural encounter occurs in which "God and man are sat down."[2] Anytime we try to program it, we automatically make the thing too small for God to fit into it.

God's presence seems to be hovering over this generation as if all time and creation are waiting and listening for something. I've often said that if a baby in a church service were to suddenly get hungry, that baby would totally disrupt the service. The frantic mother might stick a pacifier in the baby's mouth, but if that baby is *really* hungry, then that powerless piece of plastic just won't get the job done. It has no power to stifle the cry of unadulterated, unapologetic, and single-minded hunger. Only one thing will do.

At some point our churches have to get tired of preachers sticking plastic pacifiers in their mouths by talking about the *promise* of His presence. They need to set up a juvenile howl of the hungry that declares in no uncertain terms, "No, we don't want you to *talk* about Him anymore. Keep the empty promises and give us the real thing. We want to meet Him! Where do we go and what do we do?"

It happened in Jesus' ministry, and it's happening now! After the Samaritan woman at the well encountered the Living Well of God, she went back to her village to tell everyone *about* the Messiah. Once they heard about the *potential* resident in His presence, they demanded to see and meet Him for themselves. After spending two days in His presence, many of them said, "Now we believe, not because of what you said, *for we ourselves have heard Him.*"[3]

When Grecian Jews who came to Jerusalem to celebrate the Passover Feast heard that Jesus was nearby, they went to Philip and said, "Sir, we wish to see Jesus."[4] The men knew about the promise of Passover and the theology of theoretical forgiveness, but they wanted to meet Him who was the Passover Lamb. They obviously appreciated Philip's capacity to help them gain access to the Master, but they recognized the difference between a follower of Christ and Christ Himself. *This is the revolution that births revival.*

This same principle makes it difficult for me to minister to people about pursuing God and becoming God Chasers. Sometimes I get very nervous because I don't want to attract any attention to myself in the process, and I know that human nature can sometimes make that a virtually impossible task. We have the unfortunate habit of offering worship to the instrument instead of to the divine Player of the earthly instrument. And I read somewhere that "no flesh should glory in His presence."[5] I take that warning very seriously.

> We have the unfortunate habit of offering worship to the instrument instead of to the divine Player of the earthly instrument.

After a life-changing encounter with His presence several years ago, I was ruined as far as the traditional evangelistic ministry is concerned. Something was broken in me, and I just quit preaching to elicit response from men. In fact (and I don't know how to say this diplomatically), I don't really care whether or not people come to hear me speak anymore. I no longer attend church meetings to minister to people; *I go to minister to Him.* Ever since He touched me, I go to every church meeting, worship service, and prayer gathering, saying, "I wonder if this will be the night He will show up again?"

"OH, GOD, WILL IT BE TONIGHT?"

Sometimes, in the middle of my hectic travel schedule, I'll try to lie down in the afternoon for a few minutes. Sometimes I find that I can't really sleep, so I'll spend some time reading and studying the Word and then try again. Very often, I'll open my eyes and feel a deep groan in my spirit, and I'll cry out, "Oh, God, will it be tonight? Will You come to us again?"

If you think I'm strange, I can point you to the source. If you've ever had encounters with Him, then "man meetings" will drive you crazy because you will be interested only in "God encounters" after that. That is the exact name and address of my God addiction.

> The best thing we can do is to discard our programs, shred our syllabi, slide off our pews, and fall on our knees.

I don't know if that is where you live, but I am desperately hungry for an outbreak of God. I am like millions of other people around the world who are nauseated by the brand of spectator Christianity that dominates our spiritual landscape. Our modern form of "wisdom" and our heightened appetite for entertainment have overtaken the church. We've turned the worship service into a polished performance that entices the soul and fluffs the flesh (while doing nothing for the only One worthy of true worship).

I'm not special; I've just been ruined on religion. Once God "got ahold" of me, I discovered that I am interested in only one thing: I want to see the heavens break over a city. I have a strong conviction that they won't break open because of me or you; they will break open in spite of us. The best thing we can do is to discard our programs, shred our syllabi, slide off our pews, and fall on our knees.

A preacher asked me one time, "Tommy, do you really mean that?"

I said, "You don't know how much I mean that."

"You mean that if you had your way," he continued, "you would really want to turn every service into a prayer meeting?"

I said, "Oh, yes, because I have a whole lot more to say to Him than I do to anybody else." I say that because I have never yet seen, heard, or read about any preaching meeting that triggered a major outbreak of God. Preaching may have occurred in the process, but the fire broke out first at prayer meetings. It happened that way on the day of pentecost in the book of Acts, in the Great Awakenings, on Azusa Street, in Great Britain's New Hebrides Islands, and in South America.[6]

That is why I often tell people in our meetings, "If at some point the whisper of God's voice to your heart gets louder than my amplified voice up front, then just tune me out. Find a place where you can go after it with Him. If this whole auditorium turns into a prayer meeting, then it is possible that your entire city may be transformed into an altar." I confess to you that this is the very thing I'm after. How about you?

Some of us have stuffed ourselves on spiritual junk food long enough. There's an aching cry inside us for something more, but not for more of man's brand of church. I'm not an outsider casting stones at something he hasn't experienced and doesn't understand. I was raised in church. I slept underneath the church pews as a child long before there was carpet on those cold tile floors. I am four generations deep in church, but I don't know if that qualifies me for anything except to say that I don't like what I perceive man has done with church.

We Need to See Church as God Defines It

I think God's brand of church splits the heavens wide open and opens a window of glorious access between God and man. It releases such power that it starts New Testament churches and re-creates the joy, the ecstasy, and the sound and fury that the 120 experienced in the Upper Room in

Jerusalem on pentecost two thousand years ago. I don't know about you, but I can't say that I've attended a meeting like that yet, and I know I'd remember it. *Everyone would.*

I know we like to say, "Oh, yes, we want another upper room visitation!" but we go straight to the formula section again. We want the microwave recipe for revival, the "push-button presence" version supposedly produced if you mix just the right preacher with just the right singer and a liberal dose of hype to raise the people's emotions.

No, at some point we have to say to Him, "It is You that we want." Too many of us are content with the tried and proven ways of man, where we work our way into His presence with outward shows of righteousness and a secret intention of human manipulation. We are happy if He just sticks His hands out from underneath the veil to distribute our laundry list of wants, desires, and pleasant spiritual gifts. No, we are thankful for all His countless blessings, but we aren't happy with those things anymore. My cry is this: "I want to go past the veil and into the *face place,* the place of His presence."

God shows a peculiar liking for the kind of spiritual hunger that shows up outside the buildings we think are so holy.

I'm tired of dancing around in the outer court in endless celebration of the *promise* of His presence. The truth is that God has always hated veils. Veils separate Him from His children; and the first time He obtained the legal right, He ripped the veil of separation through the death of His only begotten Son. For some unfathomable reason, mankind is constantly trying to reweave the curtain of separation.

We do everything we can in word and deed to obfuscate and obliterate the path of direct access to Him. We are carefully re-creating the dividing wall of religious law. We make it difficult for anyone to find God when we say, "Oh, no, you can't do that. First you have to go here, and then you have to do this and meet this standard. Once we say you meet our standards, then we'll see about letting you go there." Above all, we try to make ourselves the New Testament version of the Old Testament priest and say, "Your only access to the Father is through me." I'm sorry, but the role of the heavenly mediator is already taken by God's Firstborn.[7]

Jesus delivered His most stinging remarks to the religious scholars and leaders of His day (pharisaic experts in the Mosaic Law), not to the sinners on the street. He told them, "It's not so bad that you don't enter in yourself, but you try to block the door so no one else can get in either."[8]

God is restless to break out in this generation, and He will do it *in spite of us* if He has to. If we fail to discard our man-programs and make room for Him in our churches, then He will break out in barrooms. In fact, God shows a peculiar liking for the kind of spiritual hunger that shows up *outside* the buildings we think are so holy.[9]

At times when I am in prayer or when I meditate on God's Word, I have some wild dreams. They are coming to me more and more: I see scenes of major sporting events attended by tens of thousands of people. When they begin the game with a token prayer or song as usual, God suddenly shows up and breaks out in the middle of that crowd without warning.

One of the things that appear to confirm my suspicion that the dreams are of God is the hunger that seems to show up on the news almost every month. There is an incredible spiritual hunger sweeping across the globe today in the form of what we call the New Age movement and other unprecedented displays of religious hunger.

ANY CHURCH THAT OFFERS THE REAL THING HAS NOTHING TO FEAR

The church has made it a priority to throw rocks at these movements, fearful that they will seduce the saved or the unsaved to follow their false teachings. My opinion is that any church that offers the Real Thing has nothing to fear from those who offer poor substitutes.

I think we should stop throwing rocks at the people in the New Age movement and offer them *bread* instead—the *bread of His presence.*[10] We don't have to call them brothers, but we are under an obligation to notice and meet their spiritual needs. If you are going to make fun of New Age people, then you should make fun of the starving children in Somalia and Ethiopia as well.

These movements are merely indicators of the spiritual hunger that exists in the world. They indicate something else as well. It is proof that the church in its present state has not been able to meet that spiritual hunger. That is the only reason so many people have been left to look for God anywhere they can. They are desperate for an encounter with the supernatural.

I have a wild idea that at some point some New Age guru will consult his crystal ball and read his tarot cards hoping to conjure up anything to confirm the reality of the spirit realm. All of a sudden, the God of eternity will appear right there in front of him.

"Oh, you are in heresy now, Tenney," you may say.

Well, I beg your pardon, but could you tell me the difference between a New Ager and a murderer? (I know that neither one would have much of a chance to meet God in some of the programmed church performances[11] we call worship.)

Saul was on his way to Damascus with murder in his heart and official arrest papers in his hand when God appeared to him in a flash of blinding glory.[12] He wasn't asking for God's presence in the right way. It is obvious that he wasn't pursuing God the way he should have; he was determined to pursue the people of God with murderous intent. Then suddenly a sovereign visitation of God interrupted his life.

Could you tell me the difference between a New Ager and a murderer [like Paul]?

Given that biblical example of God's appearance to a confirmed murderer and Jesus-hater, I find it hard to believe that God would not be interested in someone who cries out in sincere but unguided hunger, "Oh, God, if You're there . . ."

I believe He could respond to the person just as quickly as He did in Saul's life: "Okay, that's it. I'm going to show you who I am." And He just shows up.

I can almost hear the New Age guru say, "Who are You, Lord?" (I think he'll know it's God, even if he doesn't know His name yet.)

Then God will probably answer in the same way He answered Saul: "I'm Jesus. Now why are you doing this? Throw away that crystal ball; you won't need it anymore. And get rid of those tarot cards—I Am your future." The New Ager will instantly become a New Creature when he says, "Yes, Sir."

Let me say it again: anyone who has a genuine encounter with the manifested glory of God won't have to ask, "Is it really Him?" No, that former New Ager will immediately burn those tarot cards and shatter the crystal ball and say, "What do You want me to do? I've been looking for You all my life; now I just *have* to do something for You."

If the Lord's answer to Saul and Peter is any indication, He would probably say, "Preach about Me."

The next thing you know, that man will leave that encounter and immediately rent the nearest hotel ballroom and start preaching about the Jesus he met personally. If we're not careful, the religious gatekeepers will stand up and say, "I don't want any of you to listen to that upstart nobody down at that ballroom—he used to be a New Age leader, and we just have to be careful in these evil days."

RELIGIOUS AGENDAS CAN MAKE US MISS WHAT GOD IS TRYING TO DO

The truth is that we really have to be careful or our preselected religious agendas will make us miss what God is trying to do in this generation! I referred to the real-life illustration of Jesus' triumphal entry in my first book, *The God Chasers*,[13] but I think we need to look at that event once again.

At the beginning of the Passover Feast, the Jewish high priest and the whole religious order were inside the temple praying for the Messiah to come. Can you see the mental picture of these religious leaders praying inside the temple walls, "Send us the Messiah!" in the manner of Orthodox Jews? Meanwhile, He came mounted on a donkey and passed by on a road covered with palm leaves and clothing.[14]

The noise of the joyous crowd was so loud that I can imagine hearing the high priest ask one of his "deacon" priests, "Why is it so noisy outside? Go see what they are doing out there. We have political control over this area, and I don't remember issuing any parade permits. What is going on that could explain all that noise?"

The deacon-priest grabbed some of his most trusted Pharisee ushers and stepped into the street to check out the disturbance. It wasn't long before he hustled back into the inner chambers reserved for the priests and said, "Sir, it's bad. You were right; there's a parade passing by out there, and they don't even have a permit! We are in the middle of a high holy day, and even worse than that, those people are actually tearing up the church shrubbery!"

Is God Trying to Interrupt Your Sacred Religious Performance for a Visit?

The venerable chief priest interrupted the prayers of the assembly to express his religious outrage: "Don't they know what we're doing? We are locked away inside this bastion of Mosaic tradition praying for the Messiah to come! How dare they interrupt our sacred performance of priestly duty. Find out who's in charge of that outrageous display!"

I can hear the priest-deacon ask someone in the crowd, "Uh, who's in charge of this parade?"

"Well, don't look high; *look low* because He's riding on a colt. That's Him riding on the donkey."

If we are not careful, we can lock ourselves inside our church traditions, agendas, programs, and empty rituals praying for Him to come while He passes by outside our religious box! We can easily miss our moment of visitation if He doesn't come in the format that we think He should! (It is almost certain that He will.) There is only one way to avoid the error of the priests on the day of the triumphant entry: at some point we must get desperately hungry for Him.

Shall we just gather at the river? I say we jump in! The promised land is waiting!

5

WHEN DESTINY MEETS DESPERATION

NO MORE JESUS PARADES

HAVE YOU NOTICED THAT TRUE HUNGER HAS AN uncanny ability to make us genuinely real and brutally honest? Just the mention of the word *hunger* recalls the mental picture of a hungry baby who thinks nothing of disrupting a church service to display his hunger.

Jesus must have had the boldness of a hungry baby in mind when He said, "Unless you are converted and become as little children, you will by no means enter the kingdom of heaven."[1]

Hungry babies just aren't intimidated by the people around them. They put their total focus and energy on their hunger and the source of their satisfaction. At the height of their hunger, they make no room for distractions of any kind.

Would a hungry baby care if the pastor, guest evangelist, or internationally recognized world leader of great importance were sitting close enough to have his suit stained by his tears? Would that frustrated infant hesitate one second to lift his voice in hungry desperation because of the chance that he might offend the delicate hearing of the well-fed dignitary beside him?

Ask my mother, or for that matter, ask *your* mother! She will assure you that hungry babies aren't intimidated by anyone else's opinion. All they know to do is to trumpet to the best of their ability, "Somebody feed me!" No one has told them, but they instinctively understand that their very survival depends on their ability to demonstrate their hunger.

Some of us have "faked fullness" for most of our Christian lives. Whether in church or on the job, we live with a pasted-on smile, and we refuse to leave home without it. The truth is that more and more Christian "fakers of fullness" are saying, "I've had enough of that." Their inner hunger is beginning to get the best of them, and God is beginning to get interested once again. He has noticed that the repetitive falsehoods are fading away, and He's waiting for them to be replaced by a new vocabulary of honesty: "No, I am *not* all right, and everything *isn't* fine—I'm *hungry!* The truth is that I am really sick of *churchy-anity,* but I'm desperate for Him."

HIGH LEVELS OF HUNGER DISTURB OUR COMFORT ZONE

When this kind of honesty surfaces in a church service, we start to feel awkward. That is because most of us are uncomfortable with this amount of intense hunger. Why else would we click to another TV channel so quickly at the first appearance of the programs showing the starving children in Ethiopia, Guatemala, Somalia, or some other nation? We can't bear to see the swollen bellies and spindly little legs of those innocent little children. Such high levels of hunger disturb our comfort zone.

Have we become like the Laodicean church members who said, "I am rich, have become wealthy, and have need of nothing," while totally unaware that they were "wretched, miserable, poor, blind, and naked"?[2]

A deep conviction is overtaking the church—an inner knowing is growing that something is terribly wrong. We spend entire lifetimes sitting in pews but leave the four walls of our churches and make no impact on our world whatsoever. We hear sermon after sermon, countless Bible teachings, and audit hundreds of hours of vocal specials, but we still wonder if we know Him.

We are afraid to recognize and confess our gnawing hunger of the heart, and we are even more afraid of its cure—a fresh and intimate encounter with the presence of God. It's simple: God's children need more than Daddy's Word, Daddy's gifts, Daddy's daily provision, or the assistance of Daddy's earthly assistants. We need Him. We desperately long to feel His touch on our lives.

Sometimes we stumble upon a fresh encounter with Him through a divine combination of sovereign invitation and personal desperation, and at other times we come into His presence through passionate solicitation.

Some of us remember Zacchaeus from our childhood Sunday school lessons because very few sermons for "big people" feature him for some reason. He was the height-challenged business- man who climbed a sycamore tree to see Jesus (Luke 19:1–10).

Zacchaeus's friends, along with many contemporary folks who casually peruse the pages of the Bible, probably share the same thought about him: *Lucky for him that sycamore tree was there.* I am reminded that it takes longer to grow a sycamore tree than it does to grow a man, and it seems to me that our sovereign God approaches neither task lightly, casually, or haphazardly.

> How many years did the angelic gardeners tend the tree of destiny before Zacchaeus wandered over in divine frustration, hoping to see the Savior?

THE SYCAMORE ON PURPOSE

Long before Zacchaeus was born, I believe God planted a seed beside the Jericho road. Perhaps He even sent two angels to guard it. When they said, "Lord, why are we guarding this insignificant seedling?" He replied, "I don't want one camel to step on it. Make sure that no ox hoof bends it over or bruises it, and I don't want any hungry horses to eat it."

"May we ask why, Lord? Aren't there more important things to do?"

"No, nothing is more important to Me than preplanning encounters with My children." Then He added, "I can't make Zacchaeus climb the tree, but I can plant the tree. Only his hunger will cause him to climb the tree. In the meantime, My sovereignty will make sure the tree is in its place, ready and waiting for his climb to destiny."

Don't miss your moment in the Son; God has invested more than you know in you and your encounter with Him. Think about it: *How long did God cultivate the potential of that moment in the sycamore tree?* How many years did the angelic gardeners tend the tree of destiny before Zacchaeus wandered over in divine frustration, hoping to see the Savior?

> Then Jesus entered and passed through Jericho. Now behold, there was a man named Zacchaeus who was a chief tax collector, and he was rich. And he sought to see who Jesus was, but could not because of the crowd, for he was of short stature. So he ran ahead and climbed up into a sycamore tree to see Him, for He was going to pass that way. And when Jesus came to the place, He looked up and saw him, and said to him, "Zacchaeus, make haste and come down, for today I must stay at your house." So he made haste and came down, and received Him joyfully.[3]

Zacchaeus was a very wealthy social outcast. His fellow Jews viewed him as a sinner and a traitor because he collected taxes for the hated Roman conquerors. To make matters worse, he was a man of extremely short stature among a local population that was looking for every means possible to "put him in his place."

The chief tax collector probably started that day like every other day before it. Zacchaeus probably had no idea what was going on when the crowd started to pack the dirty streets of Jericho. He was just a business-man caught in a traffic jam who was trying to see what was going on.

Zacchaeus heard the commotion and followed the crowd until he saw a glimpse of Someone who took his breath away. He was too short to see over the crowd, but even that brief glimpse of His face made him desperately hungry for more.

I wonder if . . . could this man be the One they say He is? he thought as he fought for some kind of vantage point in the towering crowd.

Then the tax collector remembered the sycamore tree he had passed hundreds of times before that day. Its broad limbs overshadowed the street where the Master would pass by. Quickly he abandoned the maddening swirl of the crowd and ran ahead until he reached the tree of his memory. As he leaned against the tree in search of a solution, an odd idea formed in his mind: *No, someone of my stature in the community doesn't climb trees for anyone. Well, the truth is that someone of my stature will* never *see Him unless he climbs this tree. I'm really desperate, but how do I preserve my dignity?*

While Zacchaeus stood in the shadow of the sycamore tree debating over his dignity, the angels were cheering, "Go on; climb the tree, man! Get up there. We didn't guard this tree for fifty years for nothing. Deity over dignity!" After all the sovereign preparations for this blind date with destiny, it was no time for Zacchaeus to wrestle with his fear of public disapproval by a public that already disapproved of him.

> When humanity fell short of the glory of God, He planted another tree of inestimable worth.

The truth is that we all have "come short" of the glory of God and we cannot see Him face-to-face without divine assistance.[4] The tree of Zacchaeus was the proverbial sycamore tree of divine purpose.

When humanity fell short of the glory of God, He planted another tree of inestimable worth. The tree of destiny for the rest of us was planted on the top of Calvary, and God Himself climbed it first so it would still be standing on our day of destiny. We can't see Him from any other vantage point, but if we can just climb that tree, we'll transcend time and access His abiding presence for eternity.

I wonder how many times that sycamore tree growing beside the road would have been trampled but for the grace of God? How many times could your destiny have been short-circuited but for the providence of the Father? I read that He has made plans for you, and they are good, not evil.[5]

Something happened to me after decades of serving God and preaching what I thought was revival. Something was missing, and I had an idea it was God's presence. That was when I decided that I was tired of standing on the sidewalk watching the "Jesus parade" pass by. I became too hungry to be satisfied with church as usual. Some people may feel that they can satisfy their hunger by watching from the sidelines and patting their children on the shoulder as they point to the parade to say, "That's Him. Watch Him now as He passes by. Never forget this moment." Hunger humbled me and consumed me until I had to find a way to get more of Him than I had. A passing glimpse would not do. I had to touch something, even if it was the hem of His garment.

THE CHURCH'S FIRST "PARADE CRASHER"

I chose to take my cue from Bartimaeus, another resident of Jericho. He may have been the church's first "parade crasher." This man was excluded from most of the privileges of social and religious life because he wasn't "whole." He was considered to be damaged goods simply because he was born blind.[6]

The name Bartimaeus literally means "son of the unclean."[7] The only way he could make a living in his hometown of Jericho was through the demeaning occupation of begging. He had no future and no hope until the day the "Jesus parade" passed through Jericho. Evidently Mark (or Peter, who was Mark's primary source for the gospel)[8] knew Bartimaeus well enough to mention him by name in his gospel:

As He [Jesus] went out of Jericho with His disciples and a great multitude, blind Bartimaeus, the son of Timaeus, sat by the road begging. And when he heard that it was Jesus of Nazareth, he began to cry out and say, "Jesus, Son of David, have mercy on me!" Then many warned him to be quiet; but he cried out all the more, "Son of David, have mercy on me!"[9]

He Had to Find Someone — Anyone — with Eyes to See

Bartimaeus was sitting in the dirt on the side of the road with his cup held out as usual, while his blind eyes stared blankly into the sun. Perhaps business wasn't going very well that morning because the road traffic was down for some reason. Then his keen ears picked up the sounds of excitement and exclamation rising from hundreds of different voices just inside the city gates. Next came the muffled footfalls of a crowd on the move through the gate, barely discernible under their loud cries. Finally the beggar decided to risk the angry response he often received when he asked a question. He had to find someone—anyone—with eyes to see:

"What's all the noise? What is going on?"

"Oh, it's that guy Jesus."

"You mean *that* Jesus? Is it the Jesus from Nazareth, the One we've heard so much about?"

"Yeah, that Jesus."

Perhaps he was risking the pain of an angry blow, but he just had to press for a confirmation of some kind: "Are you *sure* it's Him?"

Are you, like Bartimaeus, saying to yourself, "If I could just know for *sure*"?

Bartimaeus didn't know for sure, but he was determined not to miss his moment. He thought, *Well, if He's this close, I have to do something to capture His attention.* He might have even issued a warning to those nearby:

> "I'm sorry, but you will have to excuse me because what I'm about to do just might embarrass you."
>
> "What's the matter, Bartimaeus? What are you going to do?"
>
> "I am not going to let Him get this close and pass me by!
>
> "Jesus, Son of David, have mercy on me!"
>
> "Be quiet, Bart! It's Sunday morning, and we have guests in town. Don't make a scene. We don't want them to think the beggars are taking over."

If Bartimaeus had listened to his friends, he would have missed his divine appointment. One cry wasn't enough. Most of us don't like living in the tension between the first cry and God's final response. The beggar's friends answered him before Jesus did. They did their best to dissuade him before destiny could transform him. If the first voice that reaches you after your first cry of hunger says, "Calm down," it probably won't be the voice of God.

The truth is that Bartimaeus's friends couldn't do for him what Jesus could. They were offended by the beggar's cries because they perceived the cries to be distracting; but the Son of God was attracted to Bartimaeus's cries because He perceived them to be worship served on a platter of pure passion.

His friends said, "Calm down. Be quiet." But passion told this lowly beggar that this was his day for a divine encounter, so his reply was, "You're not the one who is blind; you're not the

> Most of us don't like living in the tension between the first cry and God's final response.

one who needs Him. Someone said God is nearby, and I'm not going to let Him get this close and pass me by."

Jesus had entered the rebuilt city of Jericho from the other side and passed all the way through to the opposite side without being stopped by a single Pharisee, lawyer, dignitary, or other sighted person in that town. It took a *blind* man to stop the "Jesus parade," someone who had to take the word of others that Jesus was close. It took a desperate man with a date with destiny. Destiny met desperation in the dust of a roadside that day. Bartimaeus would never be the same.

Bartimaeus couldn't even see the One he was chasing. He was incapable of effectively pursuing Jesus in a physical way, yet the blind beggar became the God Catcher that day. How did he do it?

JESUS STILL STOPS PARADES TO ANSWER THE CRIES OF HUNGRY BEGGARS

He was the forgotten outcast in the pile of dust by the wayside. Most of the residents of Jericho had seen the beggar year after year, and they had become blinded to his existence. But on that day the Son of God would stop His relentless march to the cross just to answer the man's desperate cry and open his physical and spiritual eyes. Jesus is still stopping parades to answer the cries of blind and hungry beggars (*but He never stops for the proud*).

The man couldn't see where Jesus was, and in all the loud confusion of the crowd, he didn't even know which direction to cup his hands when he shouted. In desperation, he just started to cry out with raw, unrestrained hunger and passion. His friends and critics shouted at him to hold his peace, but he openly displayed his hunger and publicly proclaimed his passion even more.

Many times, in the moment of our hunger, we don't know which way to cry out, what to say, what to pray, or what to sing! Blind Bartimaeus didn't see Jesus until *after* he had received a miracle. He had to take some-body's word for it that the cause of the disturbance was Jesus and that He was close.

There may be times in your life when your spiritual "senses" seem deafened or blinded, and you won't be able to sense the nearness of God. In times of spiritual sensory deprivation, you must walk by faith and stand on His Word. You may have to take someone else's word that He is in the house. Whether it is a worship leader, a spouse, or a preacher, pay close attention when the person says, "He's close."

In that moment, reach out for Him with all the passion and hunger in your heart—"feel after Him, and find Him, though He be not far from every one of us."[10] And never underestimate the power of one moment in His presence. *Thirty seconds in the manifest presence of God turned a murderer named Saul into a martyr named Paul.* You may be on the road to an encounter with God that will alter your destiny so much that your name might as well be changed!

Never underestimate the power of one moment in His presence. Thirty seconds in the manifest presence of God turned a murderer named Saul into a martyr named Paul.

RADICAL PRAISE BRINGS RADICAL PRESENCE!

What did Bartimaeus do to arrest the momentum of the Messiah? Examine the words he sent from his heart to the ears of God. He said, "Jesus, Son of David, have mercy on me!" He *worshiped!* With all the passion, hunger, and desperation in his being, the son of Timaeus arrested the attention of God the Son. *Radical praise brings radical presence!*

Worship comes in many forms. It can touch Him through the slightest brush of a finger against the hem of a garment. It can reach Him through the hoarse-voiced cry of the vocal cords, or it can traverse time and space without a sound as a silent scream of passionate desperation from a broken heart.

In the city of Jericho, the hunger of a wealthy but rejected businessman dangling from a tree and the unashamed cries of worship from of a desperate beggar in the dust captured Jesus' heart. One was *down* and out, but the other was *up* and out. Desperate worship stops God in His tracks no matter what social strata it comes from. All are equal in His sight. If God would stop the parade of the universe long enough to change these two human destinies forever, what could He do for you?

I wish more of us in the church would get tired of standing on the sidewalk of spectator Christianity while the "Jesus parade" goes by. Somebody needs to get hungry enough to cry out. Somebody needs to get desperate enough to arrest the attention of heaven and say, "I'm not going to let You pass me by, Lord. I thank You for what You *have* done, but I'm desperate for what You *can* do."

Zacchaeus captured the attention of Jesus when his hunger made him shed his dignity and climb the tree of destiny. (Or was it that God's sovereignty captured the attention of Zacchaeus?) Either way, one sinner's life was changed for eternity at the point where sovereignty and desperation met. Zacchaeus climbed the tree, but Jesus invited Himself to the house. *God plants the tree in your life, but hunger makes you climb it.* God creates the occasion, but you must take advantage of it: "Seek the LORD while He may be found, call upon Him while He is near."[11] If you dare to climb the tree of hunger, you may not have to invite Him—*He may just invite Himself.*

Bartimaeus caught God, too, when he captured Jesus' attention. His desperate cries to the Savior forever changed his life in the true essence of a blind date with destiny. He is coming close. How hungry are you?

Father, I pray that the spirit of Bartimaeus would grip our hearts and birth desperation in our spirits right now. I pray that incredible hunger and the fire of God-ward passion would overtake and overwhelm us. We're not going to let You get this close and pass us by. We are too hungry for You; we are too desperate to hold back now. Father, we draw a line in the sand; we'll never be the same. We are hungry for You, and we cannot go back; we refuse to retreat to the closet of fear from the place of public passion.

6

WHAT DOES A HUMAN WAITER OFFER A DIVINE CUSTOMER?

WAITING IN CAFÉ HEAVEN IS NOT SPIRITUAL THUMB TWIDDLING

THE MOBILE NATURE OF MY MINISTRY REQUIRES ME TO spend a lot more time in restaurants than I would like, so I've had the opportunity to sample the service of thousands of waiters and waitresses around the world. I had my worst experience to date when I went into a restaurant recently and fell victim to the "service" of a so-called waitress who seemed to be really inconvenienced that I even showed up. (You are probably nodding and thinking of your own misadventure even as you read this paragraph.)

The service, and I am being very kind to call it that, was so bad that I finally asked my waitress, "Ma'am, do you know who pays your salary?"

She sneered and rolled her eyes before she said, "My boss."

I said, "No, people like me pay your salary. I've even been known to tip more than the cost of the whole bill—*when the service warrants it.*" I waited until she finally looked me in the eye and then said, "Ma'am, you have no idea of my ability to change your future. I could make your day. You don't know who you wait on every day, and your boss is not the one who really pays your salary. If customers don't get good service in here, then they will stop coming. Then what will you do?"

She never did grasp my point, and a lot of Christians never "get it" either. They think church is about them, so they turn church into glorified "bless me clubs" when God thinks it's a "bless *Him* club." God has this incredible idea that church is all about Him, and He can't seem to get it out of His mind.

For some reason, God actually thinks people dress up and gather together in a church meeting for *Him!* That gives new meaning to the phrase "waiting on the Lord," doesn't it?

Waiting on Him is not some kind of celestial thumb twiddling. It has absolutely nothing to do with sitting around and doing nothing. Think of all the restaurants you've visited in your lifetime and try to think of one experience that stands out above the rest. (No, I'm not talking about romantic moments, although those are wonderful.)

Most fine dining experiences include two outstanding components, or the experiences aren't so fine: good food and a good waiter. Good waiters *anticipate* the needs of customers so effectively that they don't even have to ask. It doesn't matter whether the problem involves beverage refills, dropped silverware or napkins, or the timely delivery of the bill—they take care of it all.

On the other hand, inexperienced or poor waiters who *pretend* to be good at waiting can become the most annoying nuisances in your day. How? They quickly give their true identity away because *they constantly interrupt you* at the table to say, "Do you need something?" or "May I help you?"

The sentiment is nice, but the serial interruptions are infuriating. "Pretend waiters" feel they need to make themselves known at least five times in every fifteen-minute period. It hasn't dawned on them that the customer comes to a restaurant as a desert traveler comes to an oasis— seeking a break from the fast-paced, interruption-laced existence at home, in the office, or at the plant. You find yourself in the middle of the good conversation you craved only to be interrupted for a "stop everything and take notice of me" interruption by a pretend waiter.

You may have to stop the principal purpose of

> God has this incredible idea that church is all about Him, and He can't seem to get it out of His mind.

your conversation just to tell the one supposedly waiting on you, "We are fine." You would think the person would have enough sense to see when a water or tea glass is empty or when a coffee cup needs a warm-up without interrupting someone.

Have you noticed that you rarely notice really good waiters? You hardly know they are there! If you drop your napkin, a new one just magically appears beside your plate. If a fork gets nudged out of position and drops to the floor, or if any of the beverages, bread plates, or specialty items need attention, the need is anticipated and met quietly and efficiently, almost as it happens. When I discover true waiters in my travels, I often feel the urge to seek them out and thank them for providing a precious hour of earthly peace through a relaxing and pampered dining experience.

GIFTED WAITERS MAKE YOU FEEL SPECIAL

Gifted waiters don't act as if you inconvenienced them by showing up in their restaurant or in their serving section. They make you feel special, as if you are a long-lost and beloved family member who has returned for a special reunion meal. You get the unspoken impression that no effort is too great to honor and bless you as their special guest. I don't know about you, but I throw out the tipping guidelines when I am served by true waiters. As I mentioned earlier, I often give these rare individuals a tip equal to or larger than the bill for the dinner. Why? I like to bless them because they blessed me and my guests.

Can I tell you that is also what a good worship "service" is like? The Lord loves to come to services where we anticipate His every desire and whim. He delights to see us carefully seek the guidance of the Holy Spirit in every part of the service—whether our preset song lists, order of service, or programs are disrupted or not. "I wonder if He wants that song? Should we sing this one?" If we are not careful, we can presumptively call it "good service" when we are not even good waiters.

In churches where the pursuit of God has become the chief goal, it is common to see worship teams sing one or two songs a couple of times and then sense the finger of God fall on the third or fourth song. You can almost see something register on their faces: "Oh, *that's* what He wants tonight." Then they "camp" on that particular song until the Holy Spirit moves on to something else. That kind of flexibility can play havoc with a song list, but it blesses God (which means He blesses the people).

It's a lot like trying to find the opening in heavy, room-darkening shades in an unfamiliar hotel room in the morning. Some of those rooms can get so dark that you can't tell what time of day it is. Sometimes you get out of bed and try to find the opening in the drapes by running your fingers along the pleats until you suddenly see a shaft of light. "Oh, there it is."

That is what we do in our services sometimes. We don't exactly know where the opening leading to His presence is, so we just run our hands along the pleats of the veil until we find the place where it has been freshly ripped. Then we say, "Oh, there it is. The New and Living Way, that is how we go in."

If we forget that this is all about Him, if we revert to the myth that church is all about us, then we never quite enter in and we miss the whole purpose of it all. The short version of this is that we need a perspective change.

Many of our problems stem from our inability to see things in the spirit. Great things may be occurring in the spirit realm, but we usually need a perspective change to perceive them. When something is adjusted just right, we suddenly begin to see what has always been there!

> If we forget that this is all about Him, if we revert to the myth that church is all about us, then we never quite enter in and we miss the whole purpose of it all.

AN ELEVATED PERSPECTIVE
CHANGES EVERYTHING

My youngest daughter has been flying with us since she was an "arm and lap" baby. However, the lightbulb came on, and she realized for the first time that flying literally involved going up in the air when she was about four years old. I was sitting by her when she looked out the window during takeoff. She watched while we rolled down the runway and lifted off. Then she looked down at the ground below and turned to look at me with those great big toddler eyes and said with a childish lisp, "Wook, Daddy, wook!" and turned to look out the window again.

When you take time to look down, the childlike part of you wants to turn to Him in awe and wonder to say, "Wook, Daddy! Widdle troubles, widdle problems, widdle fears."

"What is it, baby?" I said.

"Wook, widdle houses, widdle people, widdle cars."

I said, "Baby, those houses, cars, and people are normal sized; they look small because we are up high in the sky."

My daughter shook her head and said, "No, Daddy—widdle houses, widdle cars!"

It was as if she thought we had flown over some fairy-tale land where everyone was about one inch tall, and people drove tiny plastic cars and lived in miniature houses. Her natural immaturity made it difficult for me to explain what a difference in perspective does to the perception of size and distance. Instead of looking at those things at the eye level and vantage point of a forty-inch-high child, she was now looking down on them. An elevated perspective changes everything.

That is why you can come into a worship

service weighed down with big troubles and insurmountable problems and suddenly sense a change the moment you catch an "updraft" of the Spirit. When you begin to worship, you ascend to join the Object of your adoration. The Bible says God "made us sit together in the heavenly places in Christ Jesus."[1] Suddenly you find yourself soaring in His presence. When you take time to look down, the childlike part of you wants to turn to Him in awe and wonder to say, "Wook, Daddy! Widdle troubles, widdle problems, widdle fears."

What happened? When you have an encounter with the presence of God, the problems that loomed so large that they blocked out the light of hope itself suddenly seem to be so much smaller that they've lost their power to paralyze and control your life. Did the problems change? No. Your perspective changed. You now view them from the eternal perspective of heaven as God always intended.

That is what worship does for you. Your problems aren't too big—*perhaps your worship is too small.* How big are your problems? It is time to "spread your wings" in His presence and fly above them. If you can ascend high enough, your problems become small and are less significant. Why? Your heavenly Father never intended for you to dwell in the earthly realm, constantly looking at and dwelling on your problems. You were birthed for the heavenlies. In fact, you are the only creature of earth that was birthed for the heavenlies. Everything else in the earthly realm must stay in this realm. You don't belong down here, so shake off those earthly chains!

Learn How to Entertain the Presence of God

The only way to gain a celestial perspective is to host God with your worship. In other words, you must learn how to entertain the presence of God. *If you can't host man whom you can see, how well can you host God whom you can't see?*[2]

Some years ago I was invited to speak to a Chinese church in the area of San Francisco, California. The first time I went to minister there, a young Chinese-American man came to pick me up. I'd flown three thousand miles to reach San Francisco after a string of ministry stops, so I was already tired and frustrated. Then I discovered that the airline personnel had managed to break my luggage.

After we finally escaped the baggage area and settled down for the drive into the city, I told my host, "Sometime in the next couple of days before I leave, I need to pick up some new straps to hold my luggage together well enough to get home. Maybe there will be a place by the hotel where I'm going to stay."

When my polite host said in accented English, "Oh, no hotel . . . house," I was sure the trip had taken a sudden turn for the worse.

I thought, *Oh, Lord, help me!* Then I made a mental note to make a stern phone call to my secretary. She knows that I always prefer to stay in hotels so I can have solitude to prepare for ministry. It's not that I don't enjoy people's homes, but I travel too much to stay with people and remain effective in ministry. I can't constantly entertain *or be entertained*—I have no right to minister on the presence of the Lord if I don't retreat from distractions and spend time with Him.

When the car pulled up at the house, I was imagining that hundreds of Chinese believers would be waiting for me in a small room and that I would have no opportunity to recover from what had been a nightmarish trip up to that point. I am just being honest.

When I looked up, I was pleasantly surprised to see a gorgeous house with a beautiful water fountain bubbling and gurgling in the backyard. That wonderful first impression was dampened when I entered the house and was met by what seemed to be dozens of Chinese believers in the living room! I was tired, half-mad over the luggage incident, and I'd just had thoughts of a very large crowd in a house greeting me—here it was in real life. All I could think of was that I desperately needed a nap. (*A few minutes of sleep will do amazing things to your spirituality.*)

I Am Going to Teach You Something Here

When my hosts politely asked me, "Oh, you want to join Bible study?" I was honest with them. I said, "No, I want to take a nap." They graciously excused me and led me to my room upstairs. It was very nice, so I decided to delay the irate call to my scheduling secretary for a moment. As soon as I stretched out on the bed, I fell asleep.

When I woke up an hour later, the house was quiet, so I peeked out the door to see if the crowd was still there. No one was around. I opened the door and stepped out to get a drink. I stumbled over something at the door, and when I looked down, I saw two luggage straps and two tubes of toothpaste neatly arranged on the floor at my feet.

I had briefly mentioned my need for toothpaste during the drive, along with my mention of the two straps for the broken luggage. I picked up the items and said, "Now, isn't that something? I barely mentioned my need for these things, and here they are." When I put the toothpaste and straps on the bed, I sensed the Lord say to my heart, *I am going to teach you something here.*

> If you can entertain man whom you can see, there is a potential to host God, whom you cannot see.

I went downstairs and opened the refrigerator as my hosts had instructed me to do. To my surprise, I found two twelve-packs of Dr. Pepper and two half-gallons of a particular brand of orange juice that I like to drink! I said, "Boy, this is really a coincidence."

Then the lady of the house appeared and said, "Oh, Pastor, you find your drinks."

I nodded and said, "Yes, but how did you know that I like Dr. Pepper?"

"Oh, we talked to your staff. *We know what you like.*"

When I went back upstairs, I said, "God, what are You trying to teach me?" That was when He whispered to me, *If you can entertain man whom you can see, there is a potential to host God, whom you cannot see.*

That weekend was the beginning of an incredible relationship that continues to this day. In fact, whenever I preach in the San Francisco area, I often stay with my Chinese friends instead of hotels. Why? I learned that they know how to honor and to host their guests with uncommon hospitality. They totally changed my understanding of entertaining, serving, and waiting upon the Lord.

According to our North American mentality, we are hospitable when we tell our guests, "Just come in, get whatever you want out of the refrigerator, prop up your feet, and make yourself at home." I don't know about other people, but I can't do that if it isn't my home and if I don't know my hosts extremely well. The only way I'll feel "at home" is to have my hosts make it happen. That takes a bit of effort, and that also explains why I usually prefer to stay at hotels when I'm traveling. I don't like to be a burden to anyone.

The Scriptures say that Jesus performed more miracles than could ever be recorded in the books of the world.[3] I wonder how many of those unrecorded miracles were simply the side benefits enjoyed by the villages, congregations, families, and individuals who truly received and graciously hosted the Messiah?

What will happen if we ever learn how to entertain His presence by *waiting* on Him? Is there any way to measure the potential of the supernatural power of God released in His people? *If a city is to receive divine visitation, someone must learn how to host the Holy Spirit!*

Let me illustrate my point by telling you the rest of the story about my Chinese hosts. The time came when a young man in that Chinese family decided to get married. I hadn't pastored or conducted marriages for many years, but this young man called my offices and said, "Tell Pastor Tenney I going to get married. Please ask him, 'Would you come do the wedding?'"

My scheduling secretary called to pass along the message, and she said, "I don't see how you can do this." When I asked, "Who is it?" she said, "Oh, you know, the Chinese family."

Immediately I told her, "You tell them I'll be right there."

I flew to San Francisco with my youngest daughter at my own expense and did the wedding, and we had a great time. "Tommy, why would you juggle an already packed schedule and climb into an airplane for a long three-thousand-mile flight just to do a wedding?" you may ask.

You don't understand. It was in this family's home that I learned about the power of hospitality and the gift of entertaining. God used these gracious people to teach me how to wait on people and anticipate needs. *They increased my potential to wait upon Him.*

The only way we can break free from the stressing restraints of time is to put our full trust in the eternal God who lives outside the circle of time.

Waiting by its very nature involves the concept of time. We are created creatures who, in the natural, are "trapped in time." Many—if not most—of our pressures, problems, and obstacles involve time limits of some kind. The only way we can break free from the stressing restraints of time is to put our full trust in the eternal God who lives outside the circle of time.

If you know that you will reach the end of your money before the end of the month, then time is your enemy.

If your heart cries out, "*How long* before my kids come home?" then time is your enemy.

If your hopes perished in the past and your dreams died with them, then time seems to be your enemy. Time can easily become your enemy where your finances, family members, or health is concerned. If your children don't know the Lord, you might say, "I don't want them to run out of time."

Remember that God lives beyond the grip and constraints of time. If you can ever learn the process of waiting through worshiping, then you will no longer be a prisoner of time.

IT IS IN THE WAITING THAT HE ACTUALLY PROVES HE IS GOD

Everybody likes the end results of a miracle, but no one likes the waiting process. Yet it is in the waiting that He actually proves He is God in response to your absolute dependency on Him. Waiting puts you in the position to know that Satan cannot rob you, and that it is impossible for God to be "late."

> God can never be late; He does not even wear a wristwatch. He'll reach into the past to pull your promises back into your present if necessary.

When Mary and Martha sent a messenger to tell Jesus that Lazarus was deathly sick, He didn't leave for Judea until after His friend's death.[4] If you were to interview Lazarus and ask, "Lazarus, what is it like to be raised from the dead?" he would say, "Well, it's great to be raised from the dead, but that dying part . . . now that's not so great."

When we say someone is "late," we imply that the person missed something, that something is irretrievably lost. If you are so late that you miss a meeting, you will never again re-create the dynamic of that particular meeting—even if you could make all of the participants wear the same clothes and sit in the same seats they occupied during the meeting.

However, nothing is irretrievable to the arm of God. He can reach into the past and readjust it, or He can pull it into your present and say, "See there?" He is the God of yesterday, today, and forever,[5] so He can heal your yesterdays just as easily as He can heal your todays or prepare your tomorrows.

He is the perpetual present, the Eternal I Am. He is not limited to the past or the future; He lives in the constant state of being. Can I tell you what that really means to me? In the realm where Jesus lives, in the realm of perpetual life, *Lazarus wasn't dead.* His sister Martha didn't understand that, so she said, "I know that he will rise again in the resurrection at the last day."[6]

He said, "You don't get it, do you? *I Am* the resurrection."[7] In the constant state of the presence of God, your kids are already back at home with their knees tucked under your table. Your career has already been rearranged. It is in the waiting and worshiping process that He says, "Do you trust Me?"

Time is a matter of perspective. Whenever we settle down in the presence of God, we find strength to stand because we are connected to the One who holds eternity in His hand. Isaiah the prophet, the man who saw Him high and lifted up, said,

His presence is manna that must be sought and received every single day lest it become stale.

> Those who wait on the LORD
> Shall renew their strength;
> They shall mount up with wings like eagles,
> They shall run and not be weary,
> They shall walk and not faint.[8]

God can never be late; He doesn't even wear a wristwatch. He'll reach into the past to pull your promises back into your present if necessary. He'll resurrect something that you thought was forever lost, or He will even stop the rotation of the planets and the motion of the universe if it suits His purposes. He's done it before; He'll do it again! For whom does He do that? He will move heaven and earth for worshipers, skilled waiters who know how to anticipate His needs and satisfy His hunger. Can you imagine being "tipped" by God? Even His spare change can alter your future.

Remember that worship is the process of finding and being found. It is the progression of discovering His presence and of experiencing His reactive joy over being discovered!

If you come to Him hungry, He will satisfy you. If you come to Him thirsty, He will satisfy you; but He will give you only enough for today. You must seek Him for more tomorrow. His presence is manna that must be sought and received every single day lest it become stale. We've made a religion out of living on dried-out crumbs from yesterday's foray into His presence.

Take off your watch, open your heart, close your eyes, and say, "Father, I'm waiting on You. I need Your touch." Then begin to wait on Him. Worship Him!

THE 120 "WAITERS" EXPERIENCED THE MOST SIGNIFICANT "SUDDENLY" OF ALL TIME

When the 120 began the prayer process in the Upper Room, they probably thought they were conducting another one of those all-night prayer meetings Jesus held so often. One night ran into the next day, the second day, and finally to the seventh or tenth day, the Feast of Firstfruits or pentecost.[9] Then the waiting worshipers in the Upper Room experienced the most significant "suddenly" of all time.[10]

The waiting process isn't always easy, but the rewards are worth waiting for when you are waiting on God. I am not a particularly good waiter in the natural because I become impatient. However, once the Lord helped me get hungry enough to wait on Him and experience His manifest presence, I just couldn't get enough of Him. Now I am determined to wait as long as necessary to welcome His presence.

The Scriptures indicate that far more than five hundred people saw Jesus before He ascended to heaven.[11] That means they personally witnessed or knew about Jesus' command at the Ascension: "Tarry in the city of Jerusalem until you are endued with power from on high."[12]

The word *tarry* means to "delay, linger, or wait." You can't rush God, and you can't force Him to fit into some man-made schedule any more than you can force Him to fit into a shoe box in your closet. God does not conform to man's time schedule; man conforms to God.

We know from the Divine Record that by the time heaven's fire fell on the worshipers in the Upper Room and "set their hair on fire," there were 120 people in the room.[13] *What happened to the other 380 people?* They just couldn't wait. When you can't wait, you may miss your moment.

The Most Difficult Part of Revival Is the Pregnancy Stage

I've noticed that women have no problem identifying with this statement. The actual birthing stage of the pregnancy process usually comes to a climax in a matter of hours or a day at most, but it takes nine months of waiting to reach that point. Mothers who have carried a baby from conception to birth understand the sweet pain of waiting.

When Jesus said, "Tarry in Jerusalem," He was saying, "You need to become pregnant with My purpose before you can fulfill your potential." That divine principle applies to every work and purpose of God.

People who walk into the middle of worship services where serious God Chasers are seeking His face often say, "What is going on here?" They may see some people kneeling in prayer while others seek God in sitting positions. Some weep uncontrollably while sprawled on their faces as others silently stand before Him in various postures of worship.

Our problem is that we get in such an all-fired hurry to get results that we try to use man's matches to set our own hair on fire! *There is a big difference between the fire of God and the fire of man.* When the fire of God's presence descends to the earthly realm, it burns but doesn't consume. It burned the bush on Mount Sinai, but it didn't consume it. The book of Acts clearly says it descended on the heads of the diligent waiters in the Upper Room. When they came out of the Upper Room, their hair might have been on fire, but they weren't burned by it!

On the other hand, a lot of people have been burned by "the church in a hurry" over the centuries. Man's fire promotes man's methods instead of God's purpose and presence. That's why we often experience "burnout." You know men are reaching in their own pockets for matches when their words indicate the presence of a fleshly clock somewhere:

"Is this service going somewhere? We need to *do something.* I just wish we'd hurry up and get to the point."

He *is* the point. His presence is the destination.

"Well, what are we going to *do?* What's next?"

That is like standing on top of Mount Everest and saying, "Which way is up?" *One step in any direction is a step down.*

> We need to learn how to revere divine interruptions.

Time and time again I watch people worship and welcome God until His manifest presence enters their meetings—and then some of them begin to look at their watches, consult their order of service, or glance at their sermon notes and say, "Well, we've got to continue with the program now."

What program? I thought this was all about Him! Didn't I read somewhere that the first and greatest of all commandments was, "You shall love the LORD your God with all your heart, with all your soul, and with all your mind"?[14] We need to learn how to revere divine interruptions.

I understand that when He interrupts our services, we can often linger beyond the limits of physical endurance (especially for little children on school schedules and our senior members whose bodies need longer rest periods). When we grow weary in times of visitation, we should simply say, "We will need to go home to take care of the kids and put in an honest day's labor on the job. *I can't* wait *till the next time* because I want to learn more about waiting on Him."

Sometimes our greatest temptations for interrupting God's divine disruptions are rooted in some of God's best gifts. He gave us His Word and His equipping gifts (the apostle, prophet, evangelist, pastor, and teacher) to equip us for the work of the ministry and to prepare us for every good work.[15] God also gave us the seven *charis* or "grace" gifts listed in 1 Corinthians 12 to build up and "profit" everyone in the body of Christ.

OUR PRIMARY OBJECT OF PURSUIT SHOULD BE THE GIVER, NOT THE GIFTS!

We are so *blessed* by God's Word and by His leaders and charismatic gifts that we can quickly forget that church is about Him, not us. He gave us these gifts to equip us, heal us, lead us, confront us, strengthen us, instruct us, enlighten us, and inspire us in our Christian walk. However, God's gifts should never, ever, in no way whatsoever, take away or minimize our service of love to *Him*. Our primary object of pursuit should be the Giver, not the gifts!

All these things are wonderful gifts from God's hands, but none of them can compare with the glory of His face. They should compel and urge us to minister to Him and enter the intimacy of His embrace. Instead, by our actions, we "idolize" them by allowing them to move us from the place of waiting upon Him and anticipating His needs to the place of waiting for Him to give us a blessing and meet *our needs*.

We should always focus more on Daddy's face than on the gifts from

His hands. I am thankful for every single gift He gives us, but I want Him even more than His gifts. If we seek Him first, we ultimately receive both the Giver and the gifts.

NOTHING SHORT OF A STEP DOWN FROM THE BEST

To interrupt the ongoing visitation of God just to maintain a program is to step off the crest of Mount Everest so you can read a mountain-climbing manual or receive instructions on how to "reach the top." It is nothing short of a step down from the best.

Let me illustrate it this way. If I were in a hotel room far from home and had been separated from my wife and my family for some time, it would be wonderful for someone to say, "Let's surprise Tommy and send for his wife."

When she arrives and knocks on the hotel room door, I answer the door in a distracted tone: "Come on in." Perhaps I think it is the maid. I'm reading a letter from my wife, and it makes me feel even more homesick than usual. The letter even bears her fragrance, so I am too intent on that letter from home to look up.

"Just come on in. Sorry, but I can't talk right now," I say over my shoulder. *I'm going to memorize this,* I think. "Dear Tommy, I love you. I miss you . . . the kids are fine. Can't wait till I see you again." It may not mean much to others, but it is a love note from home to me.

So my wife walks in, and I don't pay any attention to her. I just say, "I have to read this. It's a letter from my sweetheart." Meanwhile, the living object of my affection is standing behind me, tapping me on the shoulder, and saying, "Hi, it's me!"

How many times has God come to visit us and enjoy our worship only to hear us say "over our shoulder" in answer to His knock, "Sorry, it's time to pull out our letter and reminisce about Daddy." *We can get so busy memorizing letters from Him that we miss our moment with Him.* Paul had this imbalance in mind when he delivered a corrective instruction about discerning the difference between the *letter* of the Word and the *Spirit* of the Word.[16] I love and believe in God's inspired Word. I immerse myself in it from Genesis to Revelation, but I don't want to put the Word of God *ahead* of the God of the Word. Remember, the "Word became flesh"![17]

God commands us to read, study, and meditate upon His Word, but understand that sometimes He wants to personally carve His initials on the fleshly wall of our hearts. When He does this through His manifest presence (as He did for Peter, Paul, and others), you won't have to worry about trying to remember it. You will never forget it.

"Waiting" involves pressing in, pursuing, pushing forward, and persistently seeking everything you know He has available.

I don't know where the other 380 believers went, but can you imagine how they felt *after* the Spirit fell on the 120 on the day of pentecost? Imagine one of them walking back into the marketplace in Jerusalem. He immediately notices that there are thousands of people laughing, babbling in foreign languages, and staggering drunkenly around the streets of Jerusalem. When he sees his old buddy Peter, he hustles over and asks him, "What happened here?" Peter says, "Man, our hair is on fire! You *missed* it . . . you left one day too soon."

How would you feel if you left "the day before the day of"? It makes me even more determined to say, "I'm going to wait on You, Lord. I want to see Your glory." That is what worship is all about: the process of waiting on Him. The pregnancy

> The pregnancy stage of revival involves waiting and worshiping. If you have made a good beginning, do not let the pregnancy of purpose turn into a miscarriage of man or an abortion.

stage of revival involves waiting and worshiping. If you have made a good beginning, do not let the pregnancy of purpose turn into a miscarriage of man or an abortion. God is tired of tapping a shoulder in vain attempts to wrestle us away from our agendas, religious ruts, and fleshly formulas for church. He's looking for a radical few who will say, "I'm going to wait on You until it all happens."

WHAT DOES A HUMAN WAITER OFFER A DIVINE CUSTOMER?

You offer Him good "service"! Offer Him persistent worship and insistent hunger that refuse to give up until He shows up, not spiritual thumb twiddling! Let me ask you something. Why did God ask Moses to hold up his hands while Joshua and the Israelite army battled the Amalekites in the valley below?[18] God fought for the people *as long as Moses maintained the posture of worship.*

If you are breathing, then you probably face some obstacles in your life. If you can worship over those obstacles, you can see God show up on your behalf. If you are a mother missing her prodigal son, then go home to that empty bed where your wayward son used to sleep. Stretch out your hands and worship over the place of opposition. Turn his empty bed into an altar and turn the tables on the adversary. Turn your health challenges into a place of worship. Turn your empty financial barns into a place of seed-sowing worship!

"What are You teaching Moses, God?"

"I am teaching him that if he can worship over the obstacle blocking his way, then I will make a way where there is no way. All he has to do is wait."

If you can learn to worship over the problem and wait on the One who is your Solution, you will see Him make a way down the middle of where there was no way.

Sometimes I encounter people in my ministry who are hanging on by their fingernails. I wish I could give them a big hug and assure them, "It's going to be all right." I know that I haven't been where they are, but I know *I've been where I've been.* Everybody is "a little bit pitiful" in the sense that we all have our places and points of pain. If we can learn to turn our obstacles into altars and worship through the night when necessary, then God will show up in His manifested glory in the middle of it.

Living Between "the Already" and "the Not Yet"

Can you sense your passion breaking out of its cage? Do you sense your spirit breaking loose from bondages old and new? The old-timers had a phrase for these moments. They called it "waiting on God." You are living between "the already" and "the not yet." *It's already promised, but it's not yet delivered.* All you can do is wait on God—and that is the *best thing to do* when you are living in the land of potential, in the in-between zone. Welcome to the holy place of collected emptiness and displayed hunger, one of God's favorite resting places.

> Waiting on you,
> Waiting on you,
> Patiently waiting on you.
> I ain't worried about the time,
> 'Cause, Lord, I seem to find
> Strength while I'm waiting on you.
>
> They that wait upon the Lord
> Shall renew their strength.
> They shall mount up with wings like an eagle.
> They shall run and not grow weary.
> They shall walk and they'll not faint.
> That's why I'm willing to wait.[19]

7

COLLECTED EMPTINESS

THE VOLUME OF YOUR EMPTINESS DETERMINES THE AMOUNT OF YOUR FILLING

THE TRUTH HURTS SOMETIMES, ESPECIALLY WHEN IT JARS our favorite ideas or displaces our most cherished public displays of religious duty, skill, or virtue. I don't mean to hurt anyone's feelings, but it appears that the real harbinger of revival is not a good preacher or a good singer—it is the amount of our "collected hunger."

The "God of More Than Enough" is inexorably drawn to the empty capacity of our growling spiritual stomachs, especially when we gather in one mind and one accord with an unappeasable appetite for Him.[1] The Bible said it in many ways. In one place the psalmist declared,

> The righteous cry out, and the LORD hears,
> And delivers them out of all their troubles.
> The LORD is near to those who have a broken heart,
> And saves such as have a contrite spirit.[2]

And Jesus said, "Blessed are those who hunger and thirst for righteousness, for they shall be filled."[3]

Church really is all about Him. It is all about worship and His presence; it is *not* about us and our need for things. It all seems to depend on how hungry you get for Him. As far as I can tell, hunger is the only thing that has the ability to predetermine how much of God you will receive. How hungry are you?

I remember the story of one hungry woman who sought divine help for her physical hunger. It happened during the ministry of Elisha the prophet, after one of his married students died suddenly and left an aching emptiness in his home. The prophet told the widow to "collect emptiness" so she could receive the maximum amount of supernatural filling:

> A certain woman of the wives of the sons of the prophets cried out to Elisha, saying, "Your servant my husband is dead, and you know that your servant feared the LORD. And the creditor is coming to take my two sons to be his slaves." So Elisha said to her, "What shall I do for you? Tell me, what do you have in the house?" And she said, "Your maidservant has *nothing in the house but a jar of oil.*" Then he said, "Go, *borrow vessels* from everywhere, *from all your neighbors—empty vessels; do not gather just a few.*"[4]

The widow didn't realize that her cumulative emptiness would literally determine the measure of her miraculous filling.

Why would God speak through a prophet and tell a widow to collect "emptiness" from her neighbors? I like the poetic way the Authorized Version puts it: "Borrow not a few." That means, "Borrow a lot of pots and pans. Get as many empty containers as you can. Collect all the emptiness you can find."

The desperate widow and mother had no idea that the volume of her collected emptiness was going to determine her future. She didn't know how it would all work out; all she knew was to obey God's command. She didn't realize that her cumulative emptiness would literally determine the measure of her miraculous filling. The prophet gave her a hint of God's supernatural response to her hunger:

"And when you have come in, you shall shut the door behind you and your sons; then *pour it into all those vessels,* and set aside the full ones." So she went from him and shut the door behind her and her sons, who brought the vessels to her; and *she poured it out.* Now it came to pass, when the vessels were full, that she said to her son, "Bring me another vessel." And he said to her, "There is not another vessel." So the oil ceased. Then she came and told the man of God. And he said, "Go, sell the oil and pay your debt; and you and your sons live on the rest."[5]

Some of us are determined to "present our fullness for God to fill." Then we complain to anyone who will listen that this "intimacy with God stuff" is a hoax. God isn't interested in meeting you at your best—*that is really when you are at your worst.* He isn't interested in blessing your independence; He responds to your dependence. His strength is attracted to your weakness. He casts down the proud, but He runs to the pitiful.[6]

God loves to pour out His fullness on man's emptiness, but this won't happen until we run out (*or willingly lay down*) our strength, resources, ideas, programs, agendas, personal charisma, and "holy hyperbole." James said we "have seen the end of the Lord; that the Lord is very pitiful, and of tender mercy."[7] God is "full of pity" or compassionate. When you present your emptiness to Him, He says,

"Uh-oh, hold on. Michael, Gabriel, I want you two to take care of everything up there; I'll see you."

"Where are You going, God?"

"I've heard something so pitiful that I can't ignore it. Their emptiness is an attraction for My fullness. It's time to fill some emptiness from My fullness."

If the miracle of the oil and the widow is a type and shadow of the way God fills all human emptiness, then it appears that you can collect emptiness from your neighbors as she did. In my mind, that is exactly what we are doing through intercessory prayer for our neighbors, schools, public officials, the government, and other nations.

We shouldn't be content merely to present our own emptiness to the Father; we need to collect the emptiness and pain of those around us—exactly as Jesus taught us to do through His own example. Didn't I read somewhere that "He always lives to make intercession for them"?[8] What do you live for? The Cross is constantly bringing up the names and needs of others to the Father, and so should we. It stands as a heavenly doorstop propping open the veil of access. An eternal, exquisitely expensive exit sign pleading in intercession for us to escape out sins.

"Do you really believe all that intercession stuff is doing any good?" you may ask.

My opinion doesn't matter; it's His opinion that counts. His Word tells us, "The effective, fervent prayer of a righteous man avails much."[9] That is like gathering up all the empty water pots you can and saying, "Look, God."

God says, "Pour out whatever oil you have. Empty yourself so I can fill you with more of Myself." *The volume of your emptiness determines the amount of your filling.* He can't fill anything more than what you present to Him.

> The volume of your emptiness determines the amount of your filling.

Our problem is our diet. We like to stuff ourselves on spiritual junk food and feast on dainty bless-me treats. That is the kind of spiritual "food" that has all the form and outward appearance of godliness, but is a standing denial of its power. When the real meat and bread of His presence is placed in front of us, we turn away from His table of intimacy to look for another "quick and easy" flesh-blessing snack at the shallow-food bar. The unpleasant truth is that God is under no obligation to feed casual nibblers at His Communion table.[10]

GOD IS LOOKING FOR REALLY HUNGRY PEOPLE

People who aren't really hungry, especially those who enter His presence fresh from the bless-me church smorgasbord, tend to sample a little here and snack a little there with extended pinkies in mock discernment. They appear to be looking for "just the right feeling" or "just the right song" to get in the mood for communion with God.

> "If you want a plastic pacifier or spiritual pabulum, you can have it. If you are really hungry, I have an infinite supply of My presence for your unquenchable hunger."

God is looking for really hungry people. He hopes to find them in the church, but if necessary, He will bypass an entire temple filled with dainty casual nibblers just to find a few really hungry people on the street, in a bar, or on the wrong side of town. *Really hungry people tend to be really desperate people.* In the natural, true hunger can turn an honest man into a dishonest man, and it can transform a nonviolent man into a violent maniac. True hunger will make you do things you never, ever think you would do (in the natural and in the spiritual realm).

Most North Americans really don't understand the power or pain of true hunger. Those who visit places where hunger haunts people twenty-four hours a day always return with a totally different view of hunger. In Somalia, Eritrea, Ethiopia, or other places suffering from the long-standing pangs of widespread famine, even the mere rumor that a food truck is coming can cause a crowd of ten thousand desperate people to gather at a wilderness crossroads. If the hungry hear that food is locked in a warehouse behind a United Nations compound, they may

risk their lives to storm the gates! Why? *Hunger*. Manners and social graces are lost in the presence of starvation.

Some of us need to forget about the opinions of others and put our hunger on display. Daddy is saying to us, "If you want a plastic pacifier or spiritual pabulum, you can have it. If you are really hungry, I have an infinite supply of My presence for your unquenchable hunger." We need to drop our adolescent arrogance and stop pretending we are full, well, and blessed. The truth is that we are hungry, weak, and desperate for God.[11]

He is just waiting for you to cry out to Him. Do you remember the gospel passage where Jesus was walking on the water, and according to Scripture, He *would have passed them by* but they cried out?[12] There is no better time than now to yield to the "spirit of Bartimaeus" and put our desperation on display without apology, explanation, or hesitation. Each of us should say, "Only one thing really matters, and I'm *going for it!* If Jesus is in the house, I'm not going to miss my moment!"

Somebody needs to do something right now to attract the attention of heaven, and it might as well be you. Forget where you are at this moment. Put your hand on your heart and say:

> "Set me on fire, God. I'm desperately dry and thirsty for You. Father, I strike the matches of desire; ignite me with Your fire and allow me to become a Holy Spirit arsonist spreading the fire of heaven to human hearts. I'm hungry for You, Lord."

Just understand that it is inevitable that you will attract some detractors any time you're trying to attract Jesus. Do you remember the first time you saw His face, the first time that you had an encounter with His presence? If you do, then you understand why people will put up with

People will put up with three weeks of bad church for just thirty seconds of His presence.

three weeks of bad church for just thirty seconds of His presence. They just keep coming in the fervent hope that somewhere, someday, man will get out of the way so they can see Him. The first time you see His face hooks you for eternity.

There is another way to "collect human emptiness" so you can receive divine fullness. It is rooted in God's law of seedtime and harvest. When a farmer prepares to plant seed in the ground, he must take seed corn off the storage shelf to invest it in the field of faith. In other words, *he creates emptiness on his shelf to create fullness in the field for harvest.*

For a while, it looks as if there is only emptiness in both places. Then the seed in the ground begins to produce seedlings, the first sign that God's universal law of reaping and sowing is still in effect. You can grow up in a major metropolis and still know that if you plant one kernel of corn from your shelf in good soil, then instead of reaping one kernel, you will harvest several ears of corn. The temporary emptiness created when you sow "what you have in your house" by faith produces an incredible filling. It is the law of the harvest, of sowing and reaping, in open display.

EMPTINESS MAKES WAY FOR FULLNESS

Ever since God "ruined me for ministry," I really haven't done any preaching. The way to describe my *new* ministry is that I attempt to import my emptiness or hunger for God and impart it to other people who are hungry for God. Somebody asked, "Do you preach?" No, I just talk about Jesus; we sing and worship; and we put our hunger on display and together try to rip the heavens open with our emptiness, our passion, and our praise for Him.

When you *collect* emptiness or *create* emptiness by sowing what you have into the promises of God, you are living between "the already promised" and the "not yet delivered." You are banking on the faithfulness and compassion of God, who always responds to human emptiness with divine fullness.

Collected hunger cries out for His filling, and our *collective* collected hunger will basically determine how much of Him we will receive. As I've said before, I've examined the history books closely, and it appears that God's manifested presence comes to the church in waves. We call them revivals or awakenings. Again, I have a strong conviction that another wave of God's manifested presence is about to hit the shore of the human race.

> He has frozen the movements of the cosmos at the sound of a worshipful prayer. He has made the dead to rise and struck down the mighty and proud in response to the fervent cry of emptiness and hunger.

It has happened before in measure, but I'm convinced that this new wave of glory has the potential to be different. God wants to break outside our centuries-old religious box. That means our hunger has to get bigger than the box. We literally must have an uncontainable hunger for Him if we ever hope to accommodate and entertain His presence.

Sometimes it seems that we have no idea what hunger does to God. Man's answer to hunger and thirst is temporary. God's answer is eternal, yet it also creates even more unquenchable thirst and a soul hunger that can never be fully "earthly" satisfied. The more we taste of His goodness, the more of His goodness we want to taste.

Collected emptiness is one of the keys to citywide and nationwide revival because our collected and collective hunger may even cause God to bend the rules of the universe. Ask Moses! Ask Hezekiah! He has frozen the movements of the cosmos at the sound of a worshipful prayer.[13] He has made the dead to rise and struck down the mighty and proud in response to the fervent cry of emptiness and hunger.[14]

We need to present *collected* emptiness because we need His *collected* fullness to bring a flood of Christ's life to the desert of human existence. Revival is not a natural process of time; revival occurs only when eternity visits time. Revival requires supernatural intervention and the suspension of natural processes because you really only have revival when "something that is dead comes back to life."

Satan wants decay to take root in your life, family, church, and city. He wants problems to overtake you and leech the life right out of you. If you can display your hunger and collect enough emptiness to create a valley of desire, it can become an incredible ocean of fullness when the water of His Spirit floods.[15] Somebody needs to get desperate enough to break the dam.

WE LIKE TO COLLECT ALL THE WRONG THINGS FOR THE WRONG REASONS

Part of our problem is that we like to collect all the wrong things for the wrong reasons. We like to collect facts about other people so we can hold their humanness over them like some kind of religious club. We also like to collect facts about God. We don't necessarily *do anything* with the knowledge; we just collect it and hold it up to Him as if it will impress Him. We listen to thousands of hours of teaching and preaching in our lifetimes, but those who know us are sometimes hard-pressed to verify we have anything life-changing to show for it.

Our churches are filled with people who could win Bible trivia contests because they are diligent fact collectors where God is concerned. Unfortunately too few of them understand the difference between knowing *about* God and *knowing God*.

Some of us are like the two women who were standing in front of me in a grocery store in a small town. They began talking about some celebrities they'd read about in the tabloids. They said, "Did you hear about *this* one? That one is having a baby, and have you heard that the other one got married a day after the divorce was final? I heard that one's got cancer."

If I didn't know better, I would have thought those women knew all those celebrities intimately. In fact, they didn't know them at all. All their "intimate knowledge" came from the supermarket tabloids! Their compulsive collection of suspect secondhand "facts" created a false sense of intimacy with celebrities. Sometimes our compulsive collection of secondhand facts about God can create a false sense of intimacy with deity.

Our written source of information about God is admittedly absolutely accurate and certified, but God never intended for us to seek knowledge of His Word apart from seeking Him personally. One should always point to the other. Otherwise we are "always learning and never able to come to the knowledge of the truth."[16]

I'm going to say it again: if sermons and songs were going to save our cities and nation, then they would have been saved a long time ago. True wide-scale revival requires a supernatural encounter with the manifested presence of God. This happens when we create and collect emptiness by diverting our hunger from man to Him. Remember, "blessed are those who hunger and thirst *for righteousness,* for *they* shall be filled."[17]

> Sometimes our compulsive collection of secondhand facts about God can create a false sense of intimacy with deity.

The spiritual atmosphere of a city is disrupted when people come to church pursuing His presence. I often feel obligated to tell people in our meetings, "You don't need my hand on your head right now. You need His hand on your heart." The laying on of hands is thoroughly biblical and proper, but when Daddy is in the house, it can be a step *down* from Mount Everest if God doesn't authorize it.

If you seek the "face place" first, the "blessing place" will almost naturally follow. Much of the

time we get so excited that we want to leave the "face place" prematurely and rob God of the glory and honor He finds so attractive. That in turn can limit the possible levels of blessings in the "blessing place" of the ministry gifts.

God's senses are dull to the supposed strengths and virtues of mankind, but He takes notice at the slightest hint of divine desperation and holy hunger in the least of us.

IS YOUR STOMACH GROWLING YET?

We are too easily satisfied with stories of someone else's encounter with Him. I'm sorry, but I'm too hungry for that. I want to have that encounter myself. If you are tired of merely hearing about the God encounters other people had, then start collecting and creating emptiness. The same hunger that drove them into His presence will transport you into His presence too. Is your stomach growling yet? Can you feel the hunger pangs starting to grow in strength and frequency?

Again, *the collected volume of your emptiness will determine the amount of your filling.* I confess to you that if there is a secret that I could leave with you in this book, it is this: your hunger will take you to places in God that nothing else can. Hunger for Him can take you higher and move His presence closer to you than you ever dreamed. By God's design, He is moved and attracted by the hunger of the human heart.

A nursing mom could more easily say no to her hungry baby than God could say no to a hungry heart. Again, His response to our hunger is clear: "Blessed are those who hunger and thirst for righteousness, for they shall be filled."[18]

God has never been impressed by our adolescent arrogance expressed through a litany of how much we have, where we have been, or what we have accomplished in His name. None of that possesses the power to split the brassy heavens or usher in the manifested presence of God. The attraction that allows you to "catch" God has nothing to do with how well you have done or how good you think you have been. It has more to do with how hungry you are. God's senses are dull to the supposed strengths and virtues of mankind, but He takes notice at the slightest hint of divine desperation and holy hunger in the least of us.

Once He stops His procession to meet you in the face place, you won't need anyone else to confirm His presence or point the way. Saul didn't have to be introduced to Jesus on the Damascus road; he knew in his heart that he was in the presence of the Lord of glory—he just didn't know by what name to call Him because man's religion had clouded the issue. He said, "Who are You, Lord?"[19]

For too long the church has trumpeted to the nations, "He's here! He's here!" when there wasn't enough of Him there to make the church discernibly different from the world. Our claims were true in the sense that the omnipresent God was present in our churches, but that is no claim to fame. His omnipresence is everywhere, even in bars and nightclubs. It's His manifest presence that we must become hungry for, those undeniable moments when you know . . . *He's here!*

CREATE A LANDING ZONE FOR GOD'S GLORY

God wants to pour out the concentrated essence of His manifested presence on us, but He is looking for a place of "collected emptiness" to fill. That is why the God-ordained vacuum of hunger in your soul helps determine how much of Him can come. I have often written and talked about the mercy seat on the ark of the covenant because the two cherubim over the top of the mercy seat paint a beautiful picture of the way unified, purified worship creates a resting place for the Lord. I call this in-between area a landing zone for God's glory.[20]

If you can visualize two worshipers facing each other with their arms extended upward and slightly angled toward each other, then you have visualized the position of the two cherubim on top of the ark. The area or space between them was called the mercy seat. When God's manifested presence comes down to us in response to our worship, He doesn't come to you on one side or to me on the other side of the mercy seat. He comes right in the middle of us. Didn't Jesus say, "Where two or three are gathered together in My name, I am there in the midst of them"?[21] He always comes in the middle, and the size of that middle space, the collected and collective sum total of our corporate emptiness, determines how much of Him comes. Wherever you gather with one or more fellow worshipers in His name, He will come in the middle of your collective emptiness.

God has always been fascinated by that *middle zone* between needy worshipers. In Moses' day, He appeared in the *middle* between the cherubim. Then Jesus died on the *middle* cross. Now He looks for those who will stand *in the gap* and lift up the collected hunger of their neighbors next door, in the city, and in the nations of the world.

When priests and ministers weep *between* the porch and the altar—or whenever and however you arrive at that *in-between zone*—you are in God's territory. That in-between zone is the landing zone for His presence—the *throne zone,* if you please!

Due to the press of our schedule, we sometimes fly our small ministry team to meetings in

> He looks for those who will stand in the gap and lift up the collected hunger of their neighbors next door, in the city, and in the nations of the world.

private aircraft. One of the things the pilots always do before we take off toward a new location is to check the airport for the length of its landing strip. Why? The length of the runway determines the size of the plane that can land. In the same way, the amount of His filling is determined by the volume of our collected emptiness, or in-between zone. That in-between zone is created by unified emptiness.

When unity can say, "We don't have enough of Him," it creates the zone for His appearing. Again, the size of that landing zone determines the amount of Him that can come. We have had visitations of God in this generation and in generations past. We have said, "God is in the place!" Yes, He was, but how much of Him was there?

WE HAVEN'T SEEN ANYTHING YET

Cessna makes some of the most popular single-engine private airplanes. It seems that we are overjoyed when the "Cessnas of God" drop down on our tiny landing strips. We shout, "Oh, God is really here!" What about the Boeing 747 jumbo jets of the promise of God's presence circling overhead? I'm convinced that we haven't seen anything yet. *God is shopping for the place of the next outbreak,* a place where He can pour out His presence in such volume and power that it will impact people far beyond the four walls of our church buildings.

How can it happen? Again, the volume of your emptiness determines the amount of your filling. If you recall, the problem wasn't how much oil or anointing the widow had in her house. Even one drop of oil would do once it was placed in God's hands. It was how much collected emptiness she had.

God has enough glory to flood the earth to overflowing. The problem isn't whether or not God is enough. The only things that determine how much oil of His presence flows among us are how empty we are and how much unity we can collect.

Can I say again that the real harbinger of revival is not a good preacher or a good singer? It is the amount of our collected hunger. I repeat, God is inexorably drawn to the empty capacity of our growling spiritual stomachs when we gather in one mind and one accord with an unappeasable appetite for Him.

When the collected emptiness of the children of Israel suffering under the slave masters of Egypt reached God's ears, He dispatched His pre-selected and prepared deliverer to them. It all happened when their collective cry met God's omniscient willingness. In the *fullness of time,* a deliverer was sent from the mountain of God to bring down the throne of man. Are you hungry enough to summon the presence of the God of More Than Enough?

Let's pray:

Heavenly Father, I thank You for what You have done, but I hunger for what You can do. I stand with mothers and fathers for prodigal children to come home. Lord, I believe that families will be restored, careers placed back on track, jobs come together, and genuine revival come to churches, homes, and schools. God, I am desperately hungry for You. I don't lift up my fullness because I have none. All I have to offer You is my collected emptiness, a holy vacuum that can be filled only by Your presence. I need You! My vessel is empty and my future is in jeopardy.

I openly display my desperation and utter dependence upon You. I humble myself and create emptiness so that You might create fullness. I anticipate the joy of a harvest of Your presence in me. Come fill me, Holy Spirit.

8

HOW TO CARRY HOT COFFEE

RETAINING THE FRESH DEPOSIT OF GOD

HAVE YOU EVER EXPERIENCED SOMETHING THAT WAS SO wonderful, extraordinary, and delightful that you never wanted it to end? Those rare moments come and go throughout our lives: the first adolescent plunge into the euphoria of puppy love; the wonder and thrill of a honeymoon with your new mate and life partner; the first moment you look into the beautiful eyes of your firstborn child.

God also creates new moments we never want to end when He walks into the middle of our worship service, prayer meeting, or personal devotional time and reveals a glimpse of His glory. How do you retain something so wonderful and so fleeting? Recently I uncovered yet another piece of the puzzle and mystery of His presence. Once again, it came through the teachers from whom I've learned the most—my daughters. This time, it was my youngest daughter.

I decided that I wanted some coffee, and I got up to pour myself a cup. Then my eight-year-old stepped up to the counter and said, "Let me pour it, Daddy. Let me pour it."

I said, "No, baby, that coffee is hot. It could burn you."

She reluctantly accepted my warning, but even while I was pouring the coffee into the cup, she presented her next idea. "Well, let me carry it to you!"

I knew this wasn't going to end anytime soon, so I said, "Okay," and made sure I didn't fill the cup as usual. (She didn't notice the difference.)

Have you ever seen an eight-year-old carry a cup of hot coffee for the first time? If you have, then you probably know that you have witnessed one of the few times that a bundle of barely controlled energy and curiosity ever slowed down to less than eighty miles per hour (outside of exhausted sleep).

Experienced coffee drinkers (especially the Louisiana breed) can drape the handle of a full cup of coffee over a finger and carry out trash while stepping over the dog, talk on the phone, teach a class, hammer nails, change diapers, or even tiptoe through a Louisiana spring downpour to reach the mailbox without losing a drop.

It is a little different the *first time,* even in Louisiana.

The first time you try to carry a cup of hot coffee, you know better than to rush out as if your pants are on fire (which is the usual traveling speed for eight-year-olds). The first step is the hardest part of the journey. Any kind of sudden start, jolt, or jerk can send that hot brew over the brim of the cup and onto your exposed flesh. Even after the first step, you shuffle along taking small, tentative steps. You quickly look down, up, over, and again at the steaming contents of the cup to make sure no obstacle or unforeseen problem ahead of you causes you to spill your hot deposit of java.

How do you carry the fresh encounter of God in your inward vessel? *How does a church body guard the divine deposit from one worship experience to the next?* How do you "take this home" in real life?

Walk carefully and be aware of His every movement in your heart. Whether you are driving your car, leading worship, preaching a sermon, or bathing your baby, if you feel Him softly tap your shoulder, then "fold up the letter" and turn to look into His face. When He invades your empty

> When He invades your empty space of hunger, turn to meet Him in your spirit. Answer His gentle summons as the young man named Samuel did.

space of hunger, turn to meet Him in your spirit. Answer His gentle summons as the young man named Samuel did; he tentatively called out into the darkness of his empty room, "Speak, for Your servant hears."[1]

The first time He tends to come suddenly. After that, you may encounter Him unexpectedly as you earnestly chase Him and seek His face. Prepare a place of hunger, desire, worship, and praise for Him, and invite Him to turn aside and dwell with you. "What do You want, Lord? How can we bless and host You tonight, Lord?"

This is how you run your fingers along the pleats of the veil between the natural and spirit realms. Suddenly your spirit finds a window, a crack leading beyond the bounds of time, space, and eternity. The sweet fragrance of the Father's divine presence will billow through as He comes close to drink in the fragrance of your sacrifice of praise. "It's You, Lord! We knew You would come again."

Make Them So Hungry for His Presence That Nothing Else Matters

Are you really serious about an ongoing habitation of the glory of God? Do you seriously believe you can literally change the environment of your home, your job site, and community? If His presence is involved, then I believe it too. Do you honestly expect to draw the lost and hungry in your family and community to Jesus Christ? It won't happen if you try to do it by cramming doctrine down their throats. On the other hand, if you can make them so hungry for His presence that nothing else matters, then I will believe it too.

If you have experienced a fresh encounter with God and received a fresh deposit of His presence, then you must walk carefully. You may eventually learn how to carry it easily, but walk carefully right now. Do you remember when He felt so close, but your "distractedness" caused you to trip over your own feet of clay and you spilled something? The moment was lost, the smoke dissipated, and all too soon it was over.

Love your friends, hug your kids, go out to eat, laugh and talk, but remember that God has deposited something supernatural in you. Walk carefully so you won't "spill" any. If you can return to your worship gathering or private devotions without spilling anything God deposited in your heart, then you won't have to start over. You can go on from this deposit of glory to the next level in Him, moving from "glory to glory."[2] The goal is to increase your capacity to carry His presence and His light into the realm of darkness.

If you are talking to your friends and you suddenly feel a wave of His presence roll over you, just stop talking and see what He wants. I stop preaching when I feel a wave of His presence, no matter how many people are watching me. That is the time to silently pray, *Do You want anything? God, You are in charge.*

Learn to carry His presence so you can become a contagious carrier. King David discovered that God's glory (represented by the ancient ark of the covenant) was meant to be carried *on the shoulders of men,* not on man-made platforms or devices.

David's first attempt to carry the ark of God's presence into Jerusalem failed because he tried to carry God's glory on a new cart drawn by oxen. His second attempt succeeded because he used the consecrated shoulders of anointed humanity to carry the ark of God's presence into the holy place he had prepared in advance.[3]

> Learn to carry His presence so you can become a contagious carrier.

We still try to carry His glory on the "ox carts" of our man-made, man-driven programs or evangelistic formulas. We prefer them because they are easier, they are more predictable, and they are softer on the flesh that dominates many of our services.

The truth is that the presence of God comes on the shoulders of men and women, and it

always has. A program will never usher the presence of God into a church. As I noted in my book on worship, *God's Favorite House:*

> When the flesh of our humanity gets lazy, we try to import or carry the things of God using no-sweat methods so we can walk along beside them and get all excited about "transporting the glory." The truth is that we don't want to sweat it out ourselves.
>
> *Are You Willing to Pay the Price for God's Presence?*
>
> Jesus Himself taught us to do exactly the opposite. He came to earth as a servant who made Himself of no reputation.[4] If you don't believe sweat has value, picture Jesus sweating it out in the garden of Gethsemane . . . Things happen when you sweat out the flesh in your hunger for the Father.[5]

All biblical worship, especially in the Old Testament, was characterized by a *sacrifice.* In the eons of human existence before the Son of God invaded our world and shed His blood to purchase our freedom, only animal blood could permit men to draw near God's presence. Now we can draw near to Him through the blood of Christ and offer Him the sacrifice of praise and present our bodies as living sacrifices.[6] God provided for us, but our obligation to present something to Him is as binding as it ever was.

The only thing hunger will recognize is the Source of its satisfaction.

If you can learn how to carry the fire of worship, God will provide supernaturally and do things you can't even imagine. Long ago, Abraham heard and obeyed God's command to take Isaac, his son of promise and child born of the miraculous, to a mountain in the land of Moriah. He told his servants, "My son and I are going to worship," and then Isaac said, "Father, we have the fire. Where is the sacrifice?" Abraham carefully replied by faith, "God will provide himself a lamb for a burnt offering."[7]

When the two worshipers offered the ultimate sacrifice of praise and worship, God met them at the altar and revealed Himself as *Jehovah Jireh,* or "Jehovah will see to it."[8] If you intend to seek holy habitation instead of visitation, learn how to walk carefully while you carry His divine deposit each day.

The only way God's presence will break out over an entire city and region is if His people learn how to entertain His presence in their undying hunger for Him and carry it with them. This kind of hunger burns so brightly that it gives no place to "respect of persons" or personal agendas. Labels and religious jargon fall away and lose their power in its heat. The only thing hunger will recognize is the Source of its satisfaction.

I have a recurring dream that some Sunday morning, the hunger of God's people will reach such white-hot levels that it will create the habitation of the Holy Spirit. That morning, all the restaurant managers in the city will wonder, *Where is the Sunday morning crowd? All this food is going to waste.*

Hour by hour goes by and not one Baptist, Methodist, Presbyterian, Brethren, Church of Christ, or Pentecostal shows up at the food bar. Why? The glory of God has broken over the city, and visitation has become habitation. Everyone is so busy dining at the table of His presence that no one even thinks about pulling up at a natural dinner table. What would happen if the glory of God broke over your entire city or region? Think of the far-reaching effects it would have on the people who live there.

Are you willing to stand in the gap until God breaks out over your city? Will you worship in the weeping zone between the porch of man and the altar of God? With one hand extended toward heaven in worship, will you extend the other in intercessory compassion toward the people of your city? Some people automatically assume that "this God Chaser stuff" is all about the selfish pursuit of just another "religious buzz." No, it is all about God and His purposes, not about us.

YOU WILL NEVER LEAVE HIS
PRESENCE UNCHANGED

God may allow us to "catch" Him, but He will never allow us to leave His presence unchanged. His glory has a way of changing and transforming mortals. Somehow we come away from these encounters more attuned to His loving compassion for the lost and hurting around us. Rather than drive us inward, His manifest presence always turns our eyes away from ourselves and toward others. It drives us beyond the four walls of our meeting halls to seek and save the lost.

Unfortunately God's visitation rarely turns into habitation because of our human tendency to immediately turn our focus away from His face to concentrate on the "good feelings" His presence creates in our bodies and souls. These side benefits are wonderful, but we must keep our central focus on God, not on the pleasant side effects of His presence.

We tell one another, "Oh, God is here! He's visiting us again." Our singers rejoice and the band picks up the pace, but all too quickly it escapes us because we don't know what He is looking for. Most who have experienced visitations ask the question, "Why won't He stay? We begged Him to stay. Why can't we keep these moments?"

The answer is simple: *We haven't built a mercy seat to hold the glory of God.* There is no place for Him to sit! What is comfortable to you and I is not comfortable to the *kabod*, the weightiness of God. We are happy to sit in our comfortable spiritual recliners all day, but the seat of God, the mercy seat, is a little different. It is the only seat on earth that can bear the weight of His glory and compel Him to come in and *stay*.[9]

I know of many cities where a measure of His glory visited and major revival broke out. Thousands of people received Jesus Christ as Lord and Savior in these cities. Many of these visitations began during an interchurch search for God's presence, with several congregations and pastors working closely together in one mind and one accord. Later, just as the visitation began to look more and more like habitation, interchurch differences turned to strife and grieved the Holy Spirit.

Anytime God visits you with a miracle, an outpouring of His Spirit, or the beginnings of true revival, the enemy will come and attempt to steal the promise and destroy the deposit the Lord gave you. A woman in Elisha the prophet's day discovered this unpleasant pattern, but her careful preparation met the enemy's attack head-on. The key is that she made room for God's presence in advance. Her example offers clues for your own preparations for the habitation of God and the enemy's attempt to kill or steal His divine deposit.

This woman was doing very well in terms of money, prestige, and importance in her social circles. The Bible calls her a "great" or "notable" woman.[10] She realized that the odd-looking bald man who passed by her house regularly was a prophet—perhaps the *only prophet* who walked in true power in her day. She persuaded Elisha to stop at her house and eat something the next time she saw him.

After that first visitation, she immediately talked with her husband and called in the carpenters and bricklayers and ordered some furniture. She wanted those visitations to turn into habitation, and no effort was too great or investment too costly. When the prophet came around again, she showed him the room she had prepared, and he decided he would accept her offer of hospitality. The next thing she knew, the one who was so blessed by her preparations announced that he was ready to bless her! (That is the way things work in God's kingdom, but sometimes we are slow to catch on.)

This woman had enough discernment to perceive the anointed mission and calling of Elisha.

She knew how to "catch" God in His promises.

She had enough wisdom to want more of a holy visitation and enough determination to follow through on her plan to entertain the prophetic presence. She knew how to "catch" God in His promises.

However, she was totally unprepared for the level of blessing and unspeakable joy she would receive from her preparation for visitation. Elisha told his executive assistant to talk to the woman who had made room for God's gift to find out what he could do for her. She wasn't interested in more favor with men or governments; this barren woman wanted what only God could give her: a son in her old age. Elisha told his assistant to call the woman into the room she had prepared for him:

> When he had called her, she stood in the doorway. Then he said, "About this time next year you shall embrace a son." And she said, "No, my lord. Man of God, do not lie to your maidservant!" But the woman conceived, and bore a son when the appointed time had come, of which Elisha had told her.[11]

HAVE YOU MADE ROOM FOR JESUS?

Would you consider remodeling your house to accommodate God? Why not? He "remodeled" His house by tearing down the middle wall of separation to accommodate you and me![12] You must make room for Him if you want visitation to turn into habitation. How many times has He visited, only to discover there was no throne of praise in which He could take His rest? Was there no pillow of worship on which He could lay His almighty head? "Foxes have holes . . . birds have nests."[13] Have you made room for Jesus?

The woman of Shunem was about to discover another benefit to making room for God. When a day of trial and tribulation came, that room she prepared for holy visitation would become a room of omnipotent intervention. The bed she prepared to provide rest for her visitor would become a bed of hope and deliverance where she could lay life's most impossible problems. You make the bed, but be careful. You may have to lie in it! Many years later, this woman's son of promise collapsed in a field under the pain of a massive brain hemorrhage, stroke, or seizure of some kind.

Has your divine promise from God dropped dead in the field of dreams? Is your hope for a miracle lingering between a comatose state and a grave of adverse circumstances? Have you watched the children God gave you slip away into sin, rebellion, or bad company while your heart broke for the hundredth time?

It is time to lay the broken, fallen, and dying things in your life on the bed of worship in the room of praise that you prepared for Him. *It isn't over until God says it is over.* This distraught mother didn't run to the leaders of the city in her crisis. She ran to fall on her knees and remind God of His promises. He sent His prophet with His supernatural response:

> When Elisha came into the house, there was the child, lying dead on his bed. He went in therefore, shut the door behind the two of them, and prayed to the LORD. And he went up and lay on the child, and put his mouth on his mouth, his eyes on his eyes, and his hands on his hands; and he stretched himself out on the child, and the flesh of the child became warm. He returned and walked back and forth in the house, and again went up and stretched himself out on him; then the child sneezed seven times, and the child opened his eyes. And he called Gehazi and said, "Call this Shunammite woman." So he called her. And when she came in to him, he said, "Pick up your son."

> It is time to lay the broken, fallen, and dying things in your life on the bed of worship in the room of praise that you prepared for Him. It isn't over until God says it is over.

So she went in, fell at his feet, and bowed to the ground; then she picked up her son and went out.[14]

Do you have a place of visitation where you can rest your dead or dying visions and hopes? Begin to prepare for His habitation now, even before He shows up. You have to create the empty space and furnish it with your hunger, your worship, and your praise. Tell yourself, "I have the promise of His Word. 'Blessed are the poor in spirit . . . Blessed are those who hunger and thirst for righteousness, for they shall be filled.'[15] You visited once, so I know You will come back again. The next time You show up, I'm going to be ready for You. I'm thankful for what You've done, Lord, but I want to see what You can do. I desire not just visitation, but holy habitation." God is about to say to someone, "Pick up your son. Come get your daughter!"

WHAT WILL HE DISCOVER THE NEXT TIME HE VISITS?

Are you ready for His visitation, Pastor? Have you prepared for the coming of the One you've asked for, sir? Have you prepared for His presence, Mom? God visited you before, and He will come again—make everything ready for the King of glory. The next time He visits, will He discover the empty space of hunger and desire you have made for Him alone?

I've revisited many historic places where God visited. Satan always tries to steal the divine deposit. In many of those places, a hungry remnant are carefully preparing a place with no agenda but their raw hunger and desperation for God. They want His fresh deposit, they are walking carefully, and they believe by faith that He will pass their way again. They are right; He will.

Part of "carrying" the glory means being willing to release other things we may think are necessary. When my daughter made her first attempt to carry that cup of hot coffee across a room, it would have been unwise for me to say, "Oh, by the way, honey, pick up some creamer, and bring me some toast too."

If she was already carrying a piece of toast in her hand, would it have been wise for her to keep that toast in her hand while trying to carry coffee for the first time in her other shaky hand? Absolutely not. It was "both hands or nothing" for her that day. God says the same thing to us when it comes to the way we handle His glory and entertain His presence. He expects us to put *both hands to the plow* or not even make the attempt.[16] The only way we can properly carry the full measure of "God's hot coffee" is to release or relinquish everything that He hasn't put in our hands in the first place. As my father once wrote:

> You are not a real soldier until you've endured the pain, the discipline, the breaking and the remaking that comes in the boot camp of relinquishment . . . Anyone aspiring to leadership in God's Kingdom must learn how to relinquish man's "stability" and embrace God's change, for He is constantly transforming His people in preparation for the great wedding supper of the Lamb. That means change will be our constant companion. Where there is change, there must be relinquishment.[17]

God expects us to put both hands to the plow or not even make the attempt.

What would we have to relinquish or give up to carry or entertain His presence? The answer is anything that turns our focus away from Him and back toward us. Some of the chief offenders that turn up in conversations with pastors around the world include religious traditions, rigid congregational or denominational worship patterns, personal habits and preferences, and fixed personal or organizational agendas.

HE IS STILL THE GOD WHO MOVES AMONG US LIKE THE WIND

God has never settled down for long in rigid and fixed places or patterns of worship. By the time that Jesus entered Jerusalem on a donkey, the Jews were continuing their worship traditions in the patterns of their fathers, even though they knew full well that the Holy of Holies was empty. The ark of the covenant had been lost generations earlier. He is still the God who moves in and among His people like the wind.[18]

We must be willing to change and relinquish control in all its forms if we want God's manifest presence to remain among us. Some of us need a miracle of God to release our grip on our families and our brethren. So be it. The alternative is to follow the path of the Pharisees and Sadducees who gathered together every Sabbath to worship and revere an empty room while turning their backs on the Lord of the Sabbath. Who wants to waste his life by worshiping the self-made god of control and manipulation in the name of "stability"?

It is difficult enough for one person to navigate her way through a cluttered room while carrying a cup of hot coffee. The problems seem to explode exponentially if you require a group of people to transport that cup of coffee safely across the minefield of toys, magazines, furniture, and slumbering pets. Yet this is exactly what God has asked you and me to do together as we seek Him and simultaneously pass through and destroy the works of the enemy. As difficult as it sounds, the possibilities are endless: "If God could ever find . . . people in a church—who will band together, the amount of power He would release to them to

> If you have "caught" Him even once in your life, then you will do almost anything to catch Him again.

dispel demonic powers would be in direct proportion to the amount of unity they achieve."[19]

God made it clear that He prefers to come in answer to the cries of *two or more* worshipers.[20] He also said His disciples (Jesus *never* recruited "church members" or "pew warmers") would be known for their love for one another.[21] That means that whether we like it or not, we have to learn how to walk in love and unity. That is the only way we will ever see God "break out" over our cities and nation. That is the "two hands on the cup"!

Many people have paid a dear price to become God Chasers because their zeal for the Lord was misunderstood and resented by others in leadership or in their local church body. Some of these people played leading roles in man's machinery, but when they embraced God's presence, they were ultimately pushed out of the embrace of their unbending brethren. I am happy to say this isn't always the case, but God is pushing the point: He wants us to choose between man's approval and His approval, between man's way and His way. It isn't an easy choice, and if it is possible, most of us do everything we can to "live peaceably with all men."[22]

The Spirit of God constantly works in us to draw us closer to the Father and pull us farther from the comfortable paths of flesh-pleasing religion. Every organized church body has its own strengths and weaknesses, and each of us must fight individual battles with our desire for comfort and the stability of predictability versus our hunger for the presence of the eternal God.

You are reading this book because there is something in you that is determined to pursue Him at any cost. If you have "caught" Him even once in your life, then you will do almost anything to catch Him again and avoid losing the fresh deposit God entrusted to your care. One of the "Holy Spirit arsonists" who helped ignite the Hebrides revival once said, *"If you ever catch Him . . . never, never let Him go!"*[23]

Hold on . . .

Father, I am pitiful; I'm running out of words, and I don't know how to do what You have called me to do.

Holy Spirit, I know there is a place of Your presence in which our lives are changed. Once we encounter You there, we will never be the same.

We call for holy habitation. We join our passionate cries with the cry of Moses: Please show us Your face!

We are passionate for one thing—You. Set our hearts on fire with hunger; make us miserably desperate for more of You. Set Your hot coal of hunger and holiness on our tongues and in our hearts. We long for You.

Let Your fire burn in our churches; let the fire blaze in our homes. It's not a man that we want; we want You, Lord. Show us Your face, God.

That first attempt to carry His fervent passion in your heart was slow and careful, but be sensitive and you can nearly sense His presence everywhere and at any time. "Practice His presence," as Brother Lawrence said in the 1500s . . . and don't spill the coffee.

9

THE SECRET OF THE STAIRS

THE BRIDE'S ACCESS TO THE HEART OF GOD

WHEN MY WIFE AND I WERE FIRST MARRIED, SHE wasn't quite used to the southern openness and hospitality common to Louisiana. One time I took her to visit a man who; according to my mother, actually taught me how to walk during my infancy. When I knocked on the front door, it was obvious that he and his wife weren't home. My wife turned around to go back to the car, and I said, "Where are you going?" She said, "They're not home, so I'm going back to the car."

I smiled and said, "Hold on . . . I know where the key is hidden." She reluctantly followed me to the hiding place at the back door and watched me retrieve the hidden house key. She was even more reluctant to enter my friend's house, but she followed me into the kitchen and watched me make coffee as if I'd lived there all my life.

To say the least, my new bride was shocked and more than a little worried about what the owners of that home might think if they found us literally making ourselves at home in their family kitchen. She kept looking at the door nervously, expecting us to "get caught" at any time while I rummaged through the kitchen cabinets and refrigerator looking for coffee filters, cups, and cream.

In a matter of minutes, the owners of that home walked through the door just as she feared, but they showed absolutely no surprise or shock that we were there. They were thrilled to find us sitting at their kitchen table sipping some hot and strong Louisiana coffee. In fact, they acted as if *we* were the homeowners and they were the visiting guests!

After a wonderful visit, we returned to the car and headed for home. That was when I explained to my bride, "It is understood in this area that if some folks tell you where they have hidden the key to their house, then they won't mind you making coffee in their kitchen." When someone shows you his hidden key, he has given you family privileges.

God has shown us His hidden key—the key to His heart and the secret place of access to divine intimacy. In the Authorized Version, Solomon called it "the secret places of the stairs."[1] It should be obvious that God doesn't mind if we enter His "house" and prepare refreshments for Him in anticipation of His manifest presence there. Especially since He's given us the key!

Unfortunately centuries of bad human decisions and our attraction to the stuff of religion muddied the waters of our privileged grace relationship with divinity. We have used man-centered, religion-based traditions and methods to rebuild the walls that divide God and man—after Jesus shed His precious blood to break them down.[2]

Some of the older church traditions implied that God is too holy, mighty, and aloof from our lowly race to fellowship with us or permit any person to come close. "The most I can hope for," a person might say, "is to find some solace in the great church buildings built in honor of His omniscience, omnipotence, and omnipresence; and pray that somehow He will see my good works and have mercy on such a worm as I."

It is true that even at our best we are rather pitiful, but that is why we are saved by grace and not by works. It is also true that God is

> We have used man-centered, religion-based traditions and methods to rebuild the walls that divide God and man—after Jesus shed His precious blood to break them down.

holy, mighty, all-powerful, all-knowing, and present everywhere. However, the word *aloof* simply does not apply to the God who came down to sacrifice His own Son on a Roman cross to restore His fellowship with our fallen race.

MODERN MAN MADE HIM BARELY GOD AT ALL

On the other side of the religious ditch, some newer church traditions seem to throw out any idea that God is holy, supremely just, and all-powerful. By the time modern man was finished with Him, He was barely God at all. The only way to manage such a magic trick is to weaken or do away with the problem of *sin,* so that is exactly what some church leaders and theologians did. As a result, many people take God's grace for granted, almost as if they *deserve* His grace. How can that make sense? *If it is deserved, it isn't grace. If it is grace, then it isn't deserved.*

> You don't need the hand of man laid on your head as much as you need the presence of God to touch your heart.

People who attempt to come to God through "greasy grace" try to slip into heaven on the "slippery slope of repentance-free salvation." They try to approach Him casually with no regard for His holiness or for their own gross sins. In fact, the word *sin* may be banned from many pulpits, and it is treated in everyday conversations as a mere religious myth of the past. Both errors in emphasis land us in a ditch and separate us from true intimacy with God.

The Creator longs for intimate fellowship

with His highest creation, *but only on His terms*. He requires total submission to Christ Jesus as Lord, genuine repentance from sin, and a proper attitude of awe, hunger, delight, and worship in His presence. In other words, *God wants us to become as little children before Him*.

The third overemphasis challenging God Chasers is the extreme focus on the blessings of God's hand rather than on the glory of His face. Many times we come to church only to present to God our long laundry lists of wants and needs. By our actions, we tell God that the whole point of our gathering is about us: our wants, our needs, and our requests for His blessing. Again, God has this incredible idea that church is all about Him! When we approach Him with the view that it is all about us, we usually end up saying, "Something doesn't feel right here. I should get a yes, but I'm hearing no." What is wrong with this picture?

I've talked about this problem in virtually every book I've written and every sermon I've delivered in recent years: We must seek His face, not just His hands. Bless the Blesser, and the blessings of His hands will come naturally.

We also have a dangerous tendency to celebrate the men and women God has blessed more than the God who blessed them. In some cases, the celebration becomes so extravagant that it borders on "the idolatry of the anointed." Perhaps we should remind people in our meetings, "Remember that you didn't come to see me; you came to see Him. You don't need the hand of man laid on your head as much as you need the presence of God to touch your heart."

I believe in the biblical practice of "the laying on of hands," but I have discovered that *His touch* is always preferred over the God-anointed touch of man. Both are good, but His touch is far better.

We "pedestalize" the prophets who can tell us the secrets of men's hearts, but where are the prophets who can tell us the secrets of God's heart? We plan our services, craft our sermons, and sing our songs to move men, but where is the church that knows how to move the heart of God?

WHERE ARE THE PEOPLE OF THE
INNER CHAMBER?

Where are the people who know Him so intimately that their worship and adoration can almost "change" His mind?[3] Where are the people of the inner chamber, the intimate companions of God who are so in tune with His heart that others seek them out for advice on how to approach the King? God wants to raise up a generation of God-pleasers, not the run-of-the-mill religious man-pleasers. Our destiny is founded upon His wisdom and purposes, not the ever-changing whims and wishes of men. That means the church desperately needs people who possess the secret of the stairs Solomon alluded to in his Song of Songs: "O my dove, that art in the clefts of the rock, in *the secret places of the stairs,* let me see thy countenance, let me hear thy voice; for sweet is thy voice, and thy countenance is comely."[4]

Later translations use other terms for this secret place, but there is something about this phrase that clearly conveys the privileged access of the lover to the Beloved. This is the path of exclusive passion, of worship reserved only for God. This is the *secret of the stairs,* the portal of privileged access enjoyed only by true worshipers. Worshipers are the one group of people we know from the Scriptures that the Father actively seeks.[5]

God talked about five men in the Old Testament who knew how to move His heart so effectively that He made statements about them to the effect, "Even if *these men* came to talk to Me about this situation, I don't think I would change My mind."

There is an underlying principle at work here. Evidently some people know how to access the heart of God so effectively and persuasively that He almost "avoids talking with them" over certain issues.

Does this sound heretical? Explain to me why God singled out five men in the Old Testament the way He did. In the book of Ezekiel, God said, *"Even if these three men, Noah, Daniel, and Job, were in it,* they would deliver only themselves by their righteousness."[6] God also declared in the book of Jeremiah: *"Even if Moses and Samuel stood before Me,* My mind would not be favorable toward this people. Cast them out of My sight, and let them go forth."[7]

Somehow these five men developed a path of secret access to the heart of God. He is saying, "There are people whom I am reluctant to talk to in times like these because I know they can move My heart. They can bring Me to the point of doing something that is different from My original intention. It is as if some people can talk Me into more things than others can." We know it as the power of prayer!

These men managed to get close enough to God to win His heart in some way. This is the power of proximity personified. We are not talking about bribery or flattery; we are talking about God Chasers who knew how to pursue Him with genuine passion in ways that drew Him close. Noah, Daniel, Job, Moses, and Samuel—they all drew close to God in spite of impossible crises and adverse circumstances.

NOAH FOUND GRACE

God had already made up His mind to destroy the human race, but then someone interrupted the divine decision for destruction. The Bible says, "But Noah found grace in the eyes of the LORD."[8] Could that also mean he looked for grace and he pursued mercy?

How did that happen? What made Noah so special? The answer is that Noah chased God in a day when *no one else* on the planet cared whether or not God even existed, and he did it at great personal cost.

When we pursue God in a slightly hostile environment, we can usually retreat to a private place of worship or prayer, but God told Noah to build a boat that was several stories high—just outside his garage in plain sight. Noah obeyed God anyway, even though it took one hundred years of backbreaking labor in a world full of critics.

Noah continued to chase God in obedience despite universal disapproval of his God project. He endured the taunts, laughter, and nonstop verbal abuse of neighbors while he constructed a boat in a place with virtually no water and absolutely no rain! It was the equivalent of building an ocean liner in your backyard in the middle of the Mojave Desert, yet Noah did it and pleased God with his sacrifice of praise through obedience. In the end, Noah's righteousness and humility before God saved his entire family and the human race as well.

DANIEL FOUND REVELATION

The persistent prayer and devotional life of Daniel is legendary among both Jewish and Christian students of the Old Testament scriptures. Never is it more clearly displayed than during his twenty-one-day fast when God dispatched an angel in answer to his prayer.

There was something about Daniel's hunger for God that brought instant response to his prayers.

The passages describing Daniel's intercession for his people reveal one of the Bible's clearest pictures of warfare in the heavenlies. We also see how closely God listens to and heeds the prayers and cries of His people.

Then he [the angel] said to me, "Do not fear, Daniel, for from the first day that you *set your heart to understand,* and to *humble yourself* before your God, your words were heard; and *I have come because of your words.* But the prince of the kingdom of Persia withstood me twenty-one days; and behold, Michael, one of the chief princes, came to help me . . . Now I have come to make you understand what will happen to your people in the latter days . . . O man *greatly beloved,* fear not! Peace be to you; be strong, yes, be strong!"[9]

Daniel, the same man who chose to seek the face of God in prayer rather than save his own life by heeding Babylon's ban on prayer, knew the power of prayer. He consistently put God first above the approval of men and even above his own safety and comfort. He also realized that his privileged access to God was meant to benefit more than just himself. He had a responsibility to stand in the gap for others, exactly as another higher and greater Intercessor would one day stand in the gap of sin for the human race.[10]

There was something about Daniel's hunger for God that brought instant response to his prayers. Maybe it was his appetite for heavenly wisdom or his humility before divinity that promoted him to the field of the five men whose words could capture the heart of God.

JOB WAS ACCEPTED BY GOD

Job was a man who passed the supreme test of adversity and demonstrated his unconditional love for God before the galleries of both heaven and hell. He became God's "poster child for God Chasers" when he proved under extreme hardship that his love was directed to the Giver of blessings, not the blessings of the Giver.

Even though Job cried out in pain and often expressed his frustration and desperation through his ordeal, he never wavered in his unqualified love for God. In the end, even after he lost his health, his wealth, his wife, and his family, he still stood firm in his love for God.

The LORD said to Eliphaz the Temanite, "My wrath is aroused against you and your two friends, for you have not spoken of Me what is right, as My servant Job has. Now therefore, take for yourselves seven bulls and seven rams, go to My servant Job, and offer up for yourselves a burnt offering; and *My servant Job shall pray for you. For I will accept him, lest I deal with you according to your folly.*"[11]

When God heard his cry and answered him, He gave Job the job of inter-ceding for his friends who had turned against him because Job was *accepted* in His sight. This is a faint but accurate type and shadow of the way God's Son would pray on a cursed tree hundreds of years later when Jesus prayed, "Father, forgive them, for they do not know what they do."[12] God listened to Job, and He listened to Jesus. We are forgiven because Jesus was accepted!

MOSES: GOD KNEW HIM BY NAME

The murderer and picture of failure God chose to deliver His people was no stranger to God's anointing and glory. Time and again, we see Moses spending long periods of time in God's smoke-obscured presence receiving the Ten Commandments, the Law, and the detailed instructions for the tab-ernacle of Moses and the ark of the covenant.

Moses saw God's power revealed in the plagues unleashed upon Pharaoh and Egypt, the parting of the Red Sea, and the destruction of Pharaoh's army. Moses ate manna from heaven and drank water from the rock of God's provision in the wilderness. Yet he also experienced the bit-ter taste of rebellion by the Israelites and his own failure when he over-stepped the bounds of obedience and struck the rock symbolizing the rock of Israel, losing his own opportunity to cross the Jordan.

It is obvious that this man knew how to talk to God, and perhaps he even knew how to *persuade* God. In the book of Numbers, God bluntly warned Moses, "Get away from among this congregation, that I may con-sume them in a moment."[13]

Moses didn't get any directive from God—instead Moses gave Aaron a directive. He told him to fill a censer with fire from the altar and incense, symbolizing repentance and worship. Because Aaron did what Moses said, the Bible says he "stood between the dead and the living."[14] As a result, hundreds of thousands of lives were saved. Moses was a man who could "capture" the heart of God.

Perhaps Moses' secret point of access to the Father is revealed in this one-of-a-kind conversation with God: "So the LORD said to Moses, 'I will also do this thing that you have spoken; *for you have found grace in My sight, and I know you by name.*' And he said, 'Please, show me Your glory.'"[15]

As I wrote in *The God Chasers,* "This burning desire to see God's glory, to see Him face to face, is one of the most important keys to revival, reformation, and the fulfillment of God's purposes on the earth."[16]

SAMUEL: HEARD OF GOD

One man in the list of five is literally named "Heard of God," and his life and ministry epitomized his name. Samuel's very conception and birth came about because his mother's desperate cry was "heard of God."[17]

In a day when few people heard from God, one desperate woman named Hannah touched the heart of God by ignoring the protests of the religious elite and crossing the gender and religious barriers erected by a dim-sighted priesthood. Her tears and utter desperation broke through the brass heavens and brought to birth the prophet who eventually anointed and guided King David.[18] Evidently she imparted her anointing to Samuel, who took it to another level.

The Bible says Samuel served the Lord in a linen priest's ephod even at a young age, and he learned to hear God's still small voice as a young boy in the temple.[19] He never forgot how to listen to and serve divinity. His relationship with God was so unique in that spiritually dry era that the Scriptures say, "So Samuel grew, and the LORD was with him and *let none of his words fall to the ground.*"[20] How many of us can make that claim today? This God Catcher knew how to touch the heart of God and change his world.

Although the life spans of these five chosen by God covered an estimated eighteen hundred years,[21] God spoke of them as if they were alive and in His thoughts that moment. Where are the contemporaries to

Daniel in our day? Why don't we hear more people saying, "I don't know about preaching, I'm not sure about singing, but if you need to move the heart of God, *you can call me*"? I believe there are people who walk in this level of intimacy with divinity right now, but heaven knows we need more of them.

Most of the time, we try to change the world through our own minuscule efforts. If you move *Him* to change the world, then the size of the "mover and shaker's shadow" cast over the problem is totally different. If God so much as "shrugs His shoulder," entire galaxies could be displaced.

Can you see why it is so important for us to draw close to Him in love and adoration? God selected five men who spanned thousands of years of human history and commented on their heavenly influence. How many would He choose today? Who are they? Where are they? We need them!

I know this much: He wants a whole host of intimates like that. He's longed for an entire nation of kings and priests and sons and daughters.

The five men seemingly hand selected by God in the Old Testament era seemed to know about and understand what Solomon called "the secret of the stairs." The men knew this secret "back stairs" access to God's presence could produce a celestial "yes" when every earthly circumstance said "no." Passionate worship will weave its way through the trappings of failure, discouragement, and difficulty to bring you to the place of passion with Him.

This is what it means to "worship until you get to the face place" or to "tarry until . . ." You refuse to stop or turn aside to celebrate when His hand of blessing "sticks out from underneath the veil."

> Passionate worship will weave its way through the trappings of failure, discouragement, and difficulty to bring you to the place of passion with Him.

You are after *more* than the blessings of His hands; you want the glory of His face. You've made up your mind and refined your pursuit to the point that you no longer seek a blessing; you are after nothing less than the Blesser.

Perhaps your mind has mounted a protest throughout this chapter. If so, please understand that logic isn't the magic key to access Daddy's heart. My girls have been "accessing my heart" since they were toddling around in diapers. Before they even developed the intellectual capacity to use logic, they were well versed in the use of passion to persuade their father.

I may not hear them say, "Play hidey-face, Daddy," anymore, but now they have developed other very effective ways to win my favor; they have moved on to the secret of the stairs.

The real reason I noticed this hidden principle isn't that I'm a third-generation minister or that I've been in thousands of church meetings around the world. I am the father of three beautiful daughters who know the secrets to unlocking their daddy's heart.

Let me be honest with you: the moment those girls start batting those big eyelashes at me, I am hopeless and helpless and in serious trouble of losing my capacity to say "no." I'm not talking about losing my ability to correct them for wrong-doing; I am referring to my ability to deny their personal requests for favors.

At this writing, I have been married for twenty-five years. That means I am totally "house-broken," and I have a personal understanding of what it means when my wife calls me "handsome" (it usually means "hand-some-over"). After years of experience, I have all the household code words down. By the same token, my daughters

> My daughters know how to push every "button" I have. They know exactly how to gain access to Daddy's favor, even in the face of stubborn resistance.

know how to push every "button" I have. They know exactly how to gain access to Daddy's favor, even in the face of stubborn resistance.

I always suspected that some kind of formal "training" was going on in the Tenney household, but my suspicions were confirmed the other day in my own kitchen.

The culprit was my middle daughter, and on that particular morning she asked me if she could do something, and I told her "no." Then she began to get pouty about it. Perhaps teenage girls don't get pouty where you live, but that morning I know of at least one girl in Louisiana who was definitely pouty.

While I stood in the doorway, my pouty teenage daughter walked over to my wife, who was drying her hands by the kitchen sink, and began to whine on her shoulders, "Dad won't let me." Then my wife said, "Let me tell you something: This is how to get your way with your daddy . . ."

I thought, *I can't believe this is happening right here in my own kitchen! I knew these lessons took place, but I thought they happened in some private room somewhere. I guess they're needed, but do they have to do it right here* with me listening?

I felt a look of incredulity creep over my face as I listened to my spouse—my partner in child rearing—say, "Now look, first you sidle up to Dad and put your arms around him. Then you kiss him on the face and make sure you tell him how much you love him." Semi-stunned, I watched as my wife gave my daughter the lesson "How to Manipulate Dad to Get Whatever You Want."

This will be interesting. In a couple of weeks or maybe even a couple of days, she is going to want something, and she'll practice this on me, I thought.

"I LOVE YOU, DAD"

She didn't even wait two minutes! She walked right over to me, put her arms around me right on cue, and said in the sweetest little-girl voice she could muster, "I love you, Dad."

I was shaking my head during the entire performance. Finally I said, "This can't be happening! You have to know that I heard everything that was just said." It didn't faze my daughter.

"I love you, Dad. [*Kiss, kiss, kiss.*] Daddy, can I . . . ?"

I can't explain what happened next, except that I opened my mouth to say "no," and "yes" came out.

Has that ever happened to you? Why did I do that? My daughter had learned how to go beyond logic and make something that was totally illogical *accessible by passion.*

If you are not in this place now, it is certain that someday you will be asking the Father for things that logic says are impossible: "That can't be revived. There is no way that can be taken care of. Don't you know you can't do this, and that request is out of the question?" At the same time, passion is saying, "I think I know a way. There is a back door, a secret stairway that can lead you there, but the only way to reach it is through passionate worship."

Obviously no one can or should even try to manipulate God to do something. However, it is also obvious to me that God "sets us up" for fresh encounters and gives us the "secret of the stairs" just to intensify and preserve our dependence upon and passion for Him.

The first line of divine encounters takes place through the wonderful pursuit of His face, when we chase Him as little children and He allows us to catch Him for a grand reunion of joy and delight. Unlike the natural progression of human children from infancy to adolescence, our position is such that we never "graduate" from this

> The second level of encounter in our journey of pursuit is the "secret place of the stairs," where we pursue Him passionately as His bride, using every means at our disposal.

level of encounter with the heavenly Father. We are to make ourselves as little children.

However, we *add* a second level of encounter in our journey of pursuit. It is the "secret place of the stairs," where we pursue Him passionately as His bride, using every means at our disposal. He gives us the secret place of access through passionate worship, but we must supply the passion and the active pursuit.

There is also a third level of encounter reserved for a time of crisis that I call "the cry God can't deny."

10

I Want You, Daddy!

THE CRY GOD CAN'T DENY

T HERE WERE TIMES WHEN ONE OF MY DAUGHTERS WAS playing hidey-face as a little diapered toddler and she would literally stumble upon a secret key to Daddy's heart. I can still remember the sound of her little bare feet running across the linoleum floor of the kitchen and onto the carpeted surface of the hallway. Then she would trip over a ravel in the carpet fibers, and I could hear a soft thud as she fell, followed by a brief moment of stunned silence. Then she would quickly suck in her breath and cry out in pain and surprise, "D-a-a-a-d-d-y!"

Can you imagine what that did to her father's heart? I didn't wait in my hiding place one second longer. It was a miracle that the closet door remained on its hinges because her desperate cry for help pulled me out of my hiding place at the speed of sound and I *ran* to meet her in her pain. Why? Her cry ended the game and brought me out.

It is one thing to enter His presence by process. It is another to be ushered in by *urgency*. When my little girl fell down, her pain short-circuited the process and suspended the game. An emergency button was pushed.

It isn't simply that she tripped on the shreds of carpet—*she cried out.* She displayed her brokenness; she gave voice to her desperation.

The Bible even implies that there is a cry that God can't deny. Abraham and Sarah waited on the promise of God for so long that they decided to "help" God along by using the womb of a hired worker to birth the promise (instead of the womb of the miraculous). We do the same thing when we turn to man-concocted revival formulas or high-powered programs to birth in a moment what God wants birthed through a "faith wait."

Sarah followed the pattern of man for her culture when she gave her maid, Hagar, to Abraham. Hagar became pregnant and bore a son they named Ishmael. He was treated like the promised son until God's promise came to pass and Sarah miraculously gave birth to Isaac. There's nothing like the real thing arriving to make the counterfeit apparent.

It took only a few years for Abraham's house to become too small to hold two "sons of promise" at the same time. Hagar and Ishmael were given a small amount of food and water and sent into the desert. Before long, the water ran out and so did hope. Hagar put her crying teenage son under a bush and moved out of earshot, praying that the Lord wouldn't let her see her son die.[1] Then the Bible says, "And God *heard the voice of the lad.* Then the angel of God called to Hagar out of heaven, and said to her, 'What ails you, Hagar? Fear not, for God has *heard the voice of the lad where he is.*'"[2]

Verbal eloquence is no match for the simple passion of a baby's cry, or the passionate plea of a broken and desperate heart. Grandiose prayers in the best seventeenth-century "King James" English could not begin to match the sheer passion of Ishmael's cry that day. Jesus said as much when He compared the simple passionate prayer of repentance by a lowly tax collector with the empty but eloquent prayer of a proud Pharisee, noting that God heard and answered the sinner while totally ignoring the hypocrite.[3] Eloquence can't be equated with automatic response!

We hear a rumor of the "cry God can't deny" during Moses' God-encounter before the burning bush. The descendants of Jacob probably

> Verbal eloquence is no match for the simple passion of a baby's cry, or the passionate plea of a broken and desperate heart.

moaned, groaned, and complained about their misery under Egypt's pharaohs for hundreds of years before Moses was born.

I HEARD THEIR CRY, SO I CAME DOWN

Yet the day came when things got so bad that the people uttered a differ-ent kind of cry. This cry had a cutting edge of desperation that possessed the power to cut through the brassy heavens over Egypt and capture the heart of God! That was when He allowed Moses to "catch" Him at the burning bush and announced, "*I heard their cry,* so I came down to deliver them out and bring them up."[4]

> I believe there are unused keys of power and divine access lying on the dusty shelves of the church that we have forgotten about.

The people of God had stumbled upon another secret key in their desperation that unlocked the heart of divinity and made heaven invade their hell.

You never know when these mysterious keys will show up. After returning home from a min-istry trip recently, I discovered that my wife had moved the junk drawer and put it in a different place. (There must be a universal rule that every house in North America has to have a "junk drawer.") I was a little upset that she hadn't checked with me before moving such an impor-tant item in our home, but I found the new loca-tion and started fumbling around through decades of collected misplacements searching for some-thing I had recently lost. That was when I noticed the huge set of keys in the back corner. My wife came into the kitchen, and I held up the huge ring of keys and said, "What do all these keys go to?"

She said, "I don't really know. Every time I found a loose key over the years, I put it on that key ring."

I was fascinated with that key collection—that key ring was big enough to make any maintenance man happy! I am convinced that our junk drawer key ring contains a key to every house we have ever lived in since we were married a quarter of a century ago. Since I have been a pastor and traveling minister from the beginning, that means there were a lot of keys on that ring. In fact, my wife and I didn't have any idea where some of those keys came from.

I believe there are unused keys of power and divine access lying on the dusty shelves of the church that we have forgotten about. Desperate passion of worship or the painful cries of crisis are going to unlock the heavens for somebody. Most of the time, we just say, "Wonder where those keys are?" It is time for us to perceive and seize the secret keys to the heart of God (and maybe clean out our ecclesiastical junk drawer!).

Frankly it is uncommon for the modern church to press through to this level of divine access. Perhaps it is because a good number of us can barely stomach a seventy-minute prayer meeting, much less a seven- or ten-day interval of intense prayer, worship, or fasting (as when the 120 "tarried" for the Holy Spirit in the Upper Room in the book of Acts).

If the determinate length of our waiting actually predetermines the size and passion of His answer, then perhaps that explains why true revival has evaded most of the church. We know that passion will cause the heart of the Father to do things that otherwise He wouldn't do, but holy desperation may even move Him more!

THAT'S THE CRY GOD CAN'T DENY!

Sometimes you come in your fullness and make yourself empty, as Zacchaeus did. At other times you cry out in your bankruptcy, hunger, and pain, and God shows up. That's the cry God can't deny. David the psalmist knew about the key of genuine brokenhearted desperation. He vividly described it for anyone who wanted to see it:

For You do not desire sacrifice, or else I would give it;
You do not delight in burnt offering.
The sacrifices of God are *a broken spirit,*
A broken and a contrite heart—
These, O God, *You will not despise.*[5]

In the early stages of writing this book, I flew to Nashville, Tennessee, to minister at a conference. My wife and I decided to bring along our youngest daughter because she liked to visit and play with the daughter of our minister friend there.

While we were at the conference, my daughter stayed at the minister's house to play with her friend, who was also eight years old at the time. The plan was that she would spend the night with her friend, so my wife and I thought we would have the evening free once the evening service was over.

After the service ended, we were getting ready to drive to a restaurant for a bite to eat before returning to our hotel. It was almost 11:30 when our cell phone rang. Our daughter was calling. My wife looked at me and said, "It's our baby. She wants us to come and get her."

Anyone who has raised children, or who is still neck-deep in the process, understands me when I say that the night had grown longer than my daughter's courage. She didn't want to spend the night at her friend's house; she wanted to come "home," and home for her in that strange city was in the hotel with Mommy and Daddy.

We were just about to leave, so I asked my assistant to take along one of our ministry interns and pick her up for me. Meanwhile, my wife settled into the backseat while still talking to our homesick little girl on the cell phone. As we drove away from the church, I listened from the front seat. My wife said, "Baby, we sent somebody to get you."

She heard her sniffle before she said, "No, Mommy, I want *you* to come get me."

The conversation kept going on and on, and I finally said, "No, I'm tired. Now, sweetheart, you tell her she will get to the hotel at about the same time we will."

At that comment, my wife handed me the phone and said, "You tell her."

So I took the phone and said, "I'll take care of this."

THEN I HEARD HER CRY

My wife had "that knowing look" that every woman seems to be equipped with. Meanwhile, I was sure I heard some of the other people in the car barely stifle a chuckle. It was almost as if they knew what would happen next.

I put the cell phone up to my ear, and I fully intended to say, "Hi, baby girl, I sent someone to get you. It's fine."

I said, "Hi, baby," and then I heard her cry and say in that "little-girl voice" with its most pitiful and teary tones, "Daddy . . . [*sniff, sniff, choke*] . . . Daddy, I want *you*. Don't send anybody else . . . I want *you* to come get me."

Everyone in the car must have been waiting for the punch line. When I said, "I'll be right there, baby," the words weren't even out of my mouth before the car rocked with laughter. What made me turn into butter and change my decision so quickly that night?

My heart didn't change because of her impeccably structured request or the sheer logic of her arguments. Logic didn't have anything to do with it, but passion and relationship had *everything* to do with it.

Passion caused God to remodel heaven so He could turn the dead-end door of death into a

It is illogical that God would sacrifice His own Son just to get close to you, but passion got in His way.

secret place of access to heaven. In His passion He said, "I have to figure out a way to get My kids in here, even if I have to remodel what was pre-existent." *It is illogical that God would sacrifice His own Son just to get close to you, but passion got in His way.*

Paul told the Ephesians that God's solution was to tear down the middle wall and remove the partition separating us from Him.[6]

Relationship and passion can make you lose all loyalty to logic. Logic clearly said, "No, you are tired, and it makes no difference who drives your daughter those few miles to the hotel. She will see you when she gets there." Yet logic was laid aside when her passionate juvenile plea bent my ear toward her. It is also the passion of a God Chaser that transforms him into a God Catcher.

Passion is illogical, but most of us began trapping our parents with our passion when we were toddling around in diapers, and some of us have continued the practice with our spouses.

REDISCOVER THE TRUE POWER OF "GOD-WARD PASSION"

After centuries of painting passion as something evil and untrustworthy, the church must rediscover the true power of "God-ward passion." I read somewhere that God's Son exhibited His uninhibited passion for His Father's house: "Zeal for Your house has eaten Me up."[7] Pardon me, but that doesn't sound very laid-back or logical to me. It sounds radical, illogical, and "over the edge" of proper religious behavior. I know this much: the religious bunch surely didn't appreciate the time God released all that pas-sion in His house; it upset a lot of "apple carts" and preestablished human agendas that day.

Again, worship is the process of discovering God's presence. If you want to find Him, you worship your way there most of the time. At times, your journey will be accelerated by passion or by your painful cries in the midst of a crisis. In those times, divinity comes in answer to the *cry God cannot deny*.

Perhaps you have gone beyond the stage of casual hunger. You have even surpassed the supercharged arena of hunger fueled by passion. You have reached the point of all-out desperation where you no longer act like yourself. You are *desperate* for an encounter at the face place. Hunger is written all over your face. You have become like Moses who said, in essence, "I'm tired of Your hands; show me Your face, Lord. Show me Your glory."

"But, Moses, you've seen the Red Sea open; you saw the plagues break the grip of Pharaoh."

"I know, but I haven't seen what I want to see—*I want You, God.*"

It takes only thirty seconds in the manifest presence of God to change the course of history for you, your city, or the nation. There is a river of tears rising across America and the world right now. This flood of holy hunger has been orchestrated by God Himself. He is determined to prepare places of divine encounter, but it is up to us to "climb the tree of destiny."

> There is a river of tears rising across America and the world right now. This flood of holy hunger has been orchestrated by God Himself.

Even though I am an ordained minister, and even though I am personally acquainted with thousands of fine ministers around the world, I must remind you that you fell in love with God—not His assistants or His gifts. You have reached the point where you can't be satisfied by the arrival of one of God's earthly assistants anymore. Your painful cry is this: "I want *You*, Daddy."

You need to put your hunger on display like a little child who is totally oblivious to the satisfied and settled people around you. Put a voice to your God-induced hunger and pain. It is time to run to

the "face place" for a one-on-one encounter with your heavenly Father. Expect God to answer when you pray, "Father, set our hearts on fire with passion."

Passionate desperation can turn God Chasers into God Catchers. You can't run fast enough to catch God, but your passionate cry of desperation, your words, can run faster than you can. This isn't an opinion; just ask Hosea the prophet. He said, "Take words with you, and return to the LORD."[8]

BRING HIM THE PASSIONATE WORDS OF YOUR LIPS

The prophet told us to take *words* with us when we return to Him. Why? Words have always been important to the One who spoke things into existence with a *word*. The Bible also says, "A good man out of the good treasure of his heart brings forth good things."[9] Never come before the King "empty-mouthed." Bring Him the treasures of your heart carefully wrapped and delivered in the passionate words of your lips—a sacrifice of praise and thanksgiving. Words can run faster than works; worship will capture what your hands can't reach.

Your works will never capture Him, but your worship, your passion, and your cry of desperation will capture His heart and usher in His presence when nothing else can.

Some of us need to make a "nagging phone call to Daddy" right now and say, "Daddy, I want *You*." It doesn't matter whether we kneel, stand, or lie prostrate on the floor. Any posture is appropriate in the passionate pursuit of His presence.

I will never forget the day I heard my aged grandmother (who has now gone home to be with the Lord) tell my father, "You'll always be my baby." (Her "baby" was about fifty-five years old at the time.)

I really understand what she meant when I look at my daughters and realize they are quickly growing up. I would play the same games with my oldest daughter that I play with my youngest *if she would let me*—the desire to play hidey-face with her is still in my heart because she will always be my baby.

When the Scriptures say we must become as little children to come to Him, it is God's way of saying, "You will always be My baby." He is always ready to play another round of celestial hidey-face with His children.

The beckoning finger of God is saying, "Come on." It is time to put a demand on the passion of God. If He ripped the veil of separation in Jerusalem two thousand years ago, then He will rip apart anything that separates you from Him now. He will rip through every obstacle in your life if you put a demand on His passion. You have no idea how much He loves you. Let your worship and hunger cry out to Him in desperation right now:

> *God, I am so sick of everything except You. I am hungry for You, and nothing else will do.*

I must warn you again that once you begin the progression of frustration, you can never return to "life as usual." It's a lot like getting pregnant. Once it happens, nothing will ever be the same. The heavens are pregnant with purpose right now because God is preparing to birth something. Men and women everywhere are saying they feel "awkward, off balance, and strangely out of place." This ungainly awkwardness of man is typical when God prepares to arrive on the scene.

> He will rip through every obstacle in your life if you put a demand on His passion. You have no idea how much He loves you.

THE CHURCH IS PREGNANT AND THE TIME OF BIRTH IS NEAR

People in every era and culture understand what happens to a woman who is nearly full term in her pregnancy. Her center of gravity has drastically changed, her balance has shifted, and she is forced to walk differently. This perfectly describes the church today. It feels off balance and awkward right now. Why? The church is pregnant with the purposes of God and the time of birth is near.

Many people may not be happy about all the changes going on. They say, "I wish we could just go back to church as usual." I'm sorry, but God's church is "expecting." She is what we used to call a "lady in waiting," and God is doing a new thing in her. Everything that can be stretched is being pushed right up to the breaking point. The church can't wear what she usually wears; she can't drink what she usually drinks. Her tastes are changing, and the food that used to satisfy won't do anymore. She craves new things, and her emotions are all askew.

Picture a water balloon that has been stretched to the breaking point. Even an inadvertent pinprick could cause it to burst suddenly. That's what the heavens are like over the church right now. One day God's people in various cities around the world will be praising Him, seeking His face, and hungering for more of His presence, and a tiny pinprick of praise or desperate worship will burst the heavens and God's glory will pour out over the earth. We really won't be able to say it was because of a man's preaching or a particular choir's singing. It will be because some desperate, passionate worshipers risked everything to break through to give their Master a drink from the well of human desperation and adoration in the House of Bread.[10]

If the determinate length of our waiting really does predetermine the size and passion of His answer, then perhaps it would help to apply this concept to our "divine pregnancy." I heard somewhere that the pregnancy of an elephant lasts two years! Perhaps that means that the "larger births" are always preceded by the longest gestation periods.

Do you feel as if you've been pregnant with the promises of God for a long time? You have done everything you know to do to bring it to pass, and now it has brought you to your knees and you are desperate. You have finally arrived in the ultimate posture of worship—*desperate despondency!*

Desperation can do what most other states of the human condition are powerless to do—it can humble our confidence in the flesh and the intellect. God gave us minds and He expects us to use them, but He never intended for them to become a wall of separation dividing Him from His children.

It took a heavenly encounter on the Damascus road to shock the logic of Saul the Pharisee into submission to the truth. For more than thirty years, this man's pharisaical head knowledge *about* God far exceeded his heart knowledge of God.

SAUL'S HEART KNOWLEDGE LEAPFROGGED PAST HIS HEAD KNOWLEDGE

Conventional logic said Saul was doing God a favor by stamping out the heretical followers of the dead Carpenter from Galilee; but in the thirty seconds he spent in the manifest presence of God on the dusty road to Damascus, Saul's heart knowledge leapfrogged past his head knowledge.

He met the *resurrected Carpenter from Galilee,* and it took three years of isolation in the desert for Paul's theology to catch up with his thirty-second experience with the Messiah in blinding

You have done everything you know to do to bring it to pass, and now it has brought you to your knees and you are desperate. You have finally arrived in the ultimate posture of worship—desperate despondency!

glory.[11] He poured out this revelation knowledge in the form of New Testament letters or epistles he wrote to the young churches in the first century. We are still feasting on the revelation knowledge Paul received in that thirty-second moment of time.

Most of us have to admit we have tried to "figure God out" and put Him in a box. It is illogical because if our efforts succeed, then He isn't God. He is larger, greater, and far more expansive than mere human logic could ever comprehend or encompass. If you ever have a genuine heart-sized encounter with Him, then your head will have to say, "I'll have to catch up later." Why? *True passion is illogical, and God's presence ignites passion.*

My passion left my logic behind during the time I was courting my wife many years ago. I attended Bible college during the day and worked a shift at a shoe store, often until 9:30 each night. I couldn't wait until the weekend to see my true love, so I used to stop at a gas station just off the interstate and call her from a pay phone.

> Passion is illogical, and passion doesn't put price limits on the cost of the encounter.

"You still up?"

"Yes, I'm up."

"Is it okay with your folks if I come over?" (She'd check it out, and if it was, I'd call my mom.)

"Mom, I'm going over to see you know who."

"Oh my, son. It is almost ten o'clock, and it takes an hour to get over there. Now you know you have school in the morning, and then you have . . ."

"That's all right, Mom. I just want to see her for a few minutes."

Exactly an hour later I was knocking on her parents' door. Thirty minutes later (it seemed like thirty *seconds*), her dad would say, "Son, it's getting late. You know how it is." Then I'd make that long drive back home (it always seemed at least twice as long on the return leg for some reason).

Was it worth it? Absolutely. Passion is illogical, and passion doesn't put price limits on the cost of the encounter. Passion says, "I don't really care."

When it's time to give birth, a woman in labor will quickly say to anyone who gets in the way or protests her "unladylike" focus on pushing her baby into a new world: "I really don't care what you think! I am not listening to what you have to say; I have one thing to do, and it is far more important than anything you have to offer at the moment."

A woman in labor has gone beyond the definition of hunger and far surpassed the meaning of passion. Now she is openly, unapologetically *desperate* to deliver her gift to the world. So it is with the people of God at the apex of the progression of divine frustration.

> Some of God's kids have tripped over a ravel in the carpet of time . . . their faces are already buried in their arms and the carpet is soaked with their tears. The more of Him they get, the more of Him they want. That is just fine with God.

SOMETHING HAS TO BREAK OR YOU WILL BREAK!

This level of the progression seems to be similar to the final stages of the birthing process. You feel a great deal of pressure, and you sense you have come to the final lap of the race. Something has to break or *you* will break. You are desperate for a breakthrough, a final point of delivery.

You are no longer interested in one-dimensional ultrasound pictures of what will come

someday. You can't bear to hear another sound recording of heartbeats coming from some unseen realm beyond the "veil" of your earthly womb. You want to experience breakthrough and hold that baby in your arms.

Don't get weary in your waiting. You are too close and too far along to back out now. Don't stop—maybe this is what it looks like right before the heavens break and He emerges through the matrix of time to manifest His glory among us.

If you are waiting on a promise from God, fan the flames of your desperation and put it on display. Make that nagging phone call to heaven and tell Him, "Daddy, I want *You!*"

Forget your dignity so you can have an encounter with His deity. Your desperation can cut through every obstacle and objection. Once the Father hears a true cry of desperation from His children, He rushes to meet them in their pain with such speed and violence that the "closet door" of His veiled hiding place is ripped in half and left behind.

The most desperate and heartsick among us will instantly embrace this message because it speaks to the pain and frustration of their "addiction" to God's presence. Some of God's kids have tripped over a ravel in the carpet of time while pursuing an encounter with Daddy. There is no need to explain the niceties of my points to these people; their faces are already buried in their arms and the carpet is soaked with their tears. The more of Him they get, the more of Him they want. That is just fine with God. It seems I read somewhere that Paul said,

> For to me, to live is Christ, and to die is gain. But if I live on in the flesh, this will mean fruit from my labor; yet what I shall choose I cannot tell. For I am hard-pressed between the two, having a desire to depart and be with Christ, which is far better.[12]

Worship is the process where we find Him in our wholeness. Brokenness is the process whereby God finds us in pieces. I am convinced that God hides when we think nothing is wrong, just to preserve the freshness of encounter. We are in our most dangerous state when we think everything is fine and we are "satisfied" with life.

God "hid" from Israel for hundreds of years after the days of Malachi the prophet. Some of God's sternest rebukes were delivered to the church at Laodicea for reasons that should make us stop and examine our own lives:

> I know your works, that you are neither cold nor hot. I could wish you were cold or hot. So then, because you are lukewarm, and neither cold nor hot, I will vomit you out of My mouth. Because you say, "I am rich, have become wealthy, and *have need of nothing*"—and do not know that you are wretched, miserable, poor, blind, and naked—I counsel you to buy from Me gold refined in the fire, that you may be rich; and white garments, that you may be clothed, that the shame of your nakedness may not be revealed; and anoint your eyes with eye salve, that you may see. As many as I love, I rebuke and chasten. Therefore be zealous and repent.[13]

God has no need to "hide" from us in our times of crises or self-cultivated hunger. When we fall into sin and hurt ourselves or grow desperately frustrated during the pursuit, God immediately shows up. The game is up because the purpose of joy is discovery, not the chase itself.

For the same reason, the Father takes joy in transforming God Chasers into God Catchers. He likes to let you catch Him! The purpose of the pursuit is the finding, not the hiding, and nothing changes the hiding into the finding so quickly as the cry God can't deny.

II

Living in the Village of Repentance at Frustration's Address

(AND CONTENT TO STAY THERE)

ONCE YOU DECIDE TO ABANDON YOUR PERMANENT place in the pew or leave that comfortable padded seat in the back of the church to chase Him, God issues a permanent change-of-address notice for you. From that moment on, you become a spiritual traveler in transit, a pilgrim on an eternal pilgrimage to the place of His presence.[1]

The problem is that the One you are chasing has never stood still long enough for man to put Him in a permanent box (although we pretend we have). It is almost like choosing to leave Egypt to chase God across the Red Sea. The initial encounter with the God of the moving cloud and pillar of fire is only the beginning.

The crossing into a chapter of life is even more miraculous and unforgettable, but there is another crossing ahead of you on the far side of a wilderness that has a test of faith attached. (And there's no turning back to the comforts and delicacies of the "Egypt" of the past.)

"But, Tommy, I don't like living with this . . . this, this *uneasy* feeling. Will I *ever* stop feeling that I need more of Him?"

Will it help if I tell you that all the spiritual luminaries of ages past have lived at frustration's address? Holy Hunger is their street in the village of Repentance, and Divine Desperation is their zip code. Their hunger was greater than their receiving, and their divine discontent made them pray a prayer like this: "Show me Your glory." They didn't base their faith on the success of their pursuit; they based their pursuit on the strength of their faith.

Repentance can accelerate the process of entering His presence. I've often said that repentance is like "worship on steroids." True repentance produces godly sorrow that bridges the gap of sin that separates us from Him. It also births desperation and brokenness.

If worship entreats the presence of God, it seems that repentance places a *demand* on His presence because He said He will not despise the sacrificial cry of a broken and repentant heart.[2]

The paper currency or dollar bills of the United States are known as demand notes. The full faith of the government backs them, and it demands a value in return. The full faith of God Himself backs His statement about repentance. It places a legitimate demand on His presence; it fuels it like pressing an accelerator on a car. Our problem is that most of us have a concept of repentance as "an occasional visit to the village of Repentance." God calls us to a lifestyle of repentance, which is living in the village.

> Our problem is that most of us have a concept of repentance as "an occasional visit to the village of Repentance." God calls us to a lifestyle of repentance, which is living in the village.

Do you feel as if you can't stand the weight of your hunger anymore? Does your frustration make you feel as if you are on the verge of depression at times? It may feel that way, but the problem is that you are disillusioned with man (probably not any man in particular) and you are sick of what we call church (although you love your local church body).

It may not look like it, but you have never been in a better place! Why? Frustration is the address to which God sends the anointing.

If you are so satisfied with everything God has done that you need and desire nothing more, then you probably won't understand much of this book.

Be thankful for every gift and blessing, but it doesn't "bless God" to act as if you've "had enough of Him." God births a frustration in your heart that compels you to pursue Him for *more and more of His presence,* which in turn makes you want Him even more! This is the only true "marriage made in heaven."

Our faith isn't based on feelings, but it *is fueled by passion.* We anchor our faith in the things God said and promised in His inspired Word, but passion provides the courage and drive to pursue and serve the God of the Word.

The Scriptures say that God works in you both to will and to do for His good pleasure.[3] His will is to draw all men to Himself.[4] We live as if the first commandment says, "Acknowledge the existence of the Lord your God and attend gatherings in respect of His power to send you to hell." It really says, "You shall *love* the LORD your God with *all your heart,* with *all your soul,* and *with all your mind.*"[5] Can you find a single laid-back, casual, coolly objective, or calm phrase in that command?

IS THIS A "CONTINUOUS AND PERSISTENT PASSIONATE RELATIONSHIP"?

Do you get the feeling something is missing from the typical Sunday morning religious experience we call church? It is God who placed this incredible hunger and divine discontent in you. Even as He blesses you, He ignites a deep hunger and longing in your heart of hearts that cries out, "Daddy, don't send Your assistant. I want *You!*"

God isn't calling us into an intellectual dialogue, although He does interact with the intellect He gave us. He is calling us into a continuous and persistent passionate relationship that He characterized as a marriage between a heavenly Bridegroom and His bride, the church.

Platonic or passionless relationships are a Greek idea; the passionate lifelong relationship of husband and wife was God's idea. Which one did God choose as a model for His relationship with the church? (Which one do we most accurately model in our church services?)

We are called into a life of dynamic, real-life faith punctuated by alternate waves of nearly unbearable spiritual hunger and the unspeakable joy of His intimate answer to our hunger. I call this state of God-ordained tension "living at frustration's address on Holy Hunger Street in Divine Desperation."

The chase can take you into some of the most challenging circumstances you will ever experience because worship takes you somewhere that you can't go otherwise. It is what you do in those circumstantial moments of divine frustration that determines whether you remain a God Chaser or you become a God Catcher. The first is good, but the second is better; and the truth is that God will constantly move us from the role of chaser to catcher and then to chaser again. After all, we serve a God who moves (and hides).

Ask Brother Silas where the chase can lead you and what worship can do for you. Brother Silas signed on to be the assistant minister to the celebrated crusade evangelist Paul. Silas was already a respected prophet in the Jerusalem church, and he had worked well with Paul in other churches. They planned to preach a crusade in Philippi in Macedonia, and Silas was excited about the prospects. After all, it was the crusade arranged after Paul received his "Macedonian vision." Surely God was going to do great things! Then they entered the holy frustration zone.

> It is what you do in . . . moments of divine frustration that determines whether you remain a God Chaser or you become a God Catcher.

WELCOME TO THE HOLY FRUSTRATION ZONE

All hell broke loose when they stepped out in faith to obey Paul's heavenly vision. On the way to the crusade, Paul interrupted the trip to cast a

demon out of a young woman who had been stalking them for days. That angered the local businessmen so much that they started a riot and nearly got Silas and Paul killed!

Instead of preaching the gospel from a crusade platform with signs and wonders following, Paul and Silas were thrown into the damp dungeon of a Philippian prison and chained to some stocks with the blows of a whip following.[6] At that point, I can imagine Silas the prophet thinking it was appropriate to ask Paul the apostle some questions.

"Okay, Paul, so what do we do now that we are in prison?"

"We do the same thing we were going to do on that crusade platform, Silas. Worship."

[In the natural, this was a great time to get frustrated and discouraged. However, if you want to be a God Catcher, then you must get to the point where circumstances don't dictate to you; you dictate to circumstances!]

"Paul, did they hit you as hard with that stick as they did me? My back is hurting, my hands are in chains, my feet are in stocks, and my head feels like it's in two places at once.

"It's midnight, Paul. I don't have to look at my Timex to tell you it's midnight. Just look at how dark it is in here . . . Paul, are you there?"

[If you can get to the point where you can worship at midnight, in physical and mental darkness that is so thick that you can't see your hand in front of your face or see any hope for the future in all your pain and confusion, then you can rise above your circumstances.]

"Don't scare me like that, Paul. They really hit me hard, and my back is hurting."

"That's okay, Silas. Let's sing."

"Paul, you can't sing very well. In fact, you are a terrible singer."

"Well, I know, but I'm hurting too."

[What does it take to worship at midnight? It means you must worship through your pain. It means you must look beyond the physical or spiritual handcuffs, open wounds, and the crushing weight of seemingly impossible circumstances to seek His face. Don't put handcuffs on yourself by worrying more about the opinions of those sitting beside you, living with you, or working near you than about the opinion of the One standing above you. Sometimes you have to forget about everyone else so you can focus on and connect with Him.]

"Silas, what are we going to sing?"

"I don't know."

"Silas, I brought you along to lead the singing—now you've got to help me sing."

"I'm hurting."

Perhaps your heart is broken and your body is aching right now. Things just aren't going right in your life, and you wish with everything in you that your circumstances were different.

I am reminded that tears are tears, whether they fall on silk pillows or worn-out linen bedsheets. Pain comes into everyone's life. The sun shines and the rain falls on the rich and the poor and the good and the bad.[7]

Pain is pain, but if you can seek Him in the darkness of your midnight, your pain can become the wind beneath your wings that lifts you into His presence!

When you came to the Lord, did you come to Him because things were going so well in your life that you just had to find somebody you could thank? (I didn't think so.) Many—if not most—of us came to the Lord because something was going bad or fading from our lives and we had nowhere else to turn.

> Pain is pain,
> but if you
> can seek Him
> in the darkness
> of your
> midnight,
> your pain can
> become the wind
> beneath your
> wings
> that lifts
> you into
> His presence!

We Try to Avoid What God Runs To

Pain and brokenness probably brought you to Him in the first place, and pain and brokenness will certainly lead you back to Him without fail. Have you noticed that *the thing God runs to is the very thing we run from?* "The LORD is near to those who have a broken heart" (and we do everything we can to avoid the pain of brokenness).[8]

Brokenness can come through catastrophic sorrow, calamity, or sin. It also can come through our determination to seek Him, obey Him, and dare impossible things at His prompting. That is contrived brokenness and self-imposed humbling. Fasting is one way to do this.

Paul was a God Chaser who was always looking for the next place God would break out over a city and nation. His compulsive addiction to pursue God and His purposes made him well acquainted with brokenness. This is his travelogue in just one chapter of the book of Acts: *"They were forbidden by the Holy Spirit to preach the word in Asia . . .* They tried to go into Bithynia, *but the Spirit did not permit them . . . After he had seen the vision, immediately we sought to go to Macedonia, concluding that the Lord had called us to preach the gospel to them."*[9]

This is the pattern of a chronic God Chaser. Paul was well practiced in the art of "running his fingers endlessly over the folds of the veil" for the latest place of access to divinity. This man lived with divine discontent.

"Wait a minute. Didn't Paul say he had learned to be content in any state or condition?" you may ask. Yes, he did. He also went on to define what he meant by being "content": "Not that I speak in regard to need, for I have learned in whatever state I am, to be content: I know how to be abased, and I know how to abound. Everywhere and in all things *I have learned both to be full and to be hungry,* both *to abound and to suffer need."*[10]

Paul lived in a constant state of godly tension and divine discontent. He expressed his unwavering hunger for God in the midst of a life littered with constant adversity and impossible obstacles. He repeatedly followed the Lord to the very gates of death and worshiped Him every step of the way.

This Pharisee-turned-apostle was a chronic God Chaser who constantly reached out for more of God, for more souls, and for more victory over the arrayed forces of darkness. His life was a great search for one more encounter with God and one more opportunity to please and worship the One who died for him. His writings express a rich rhetoric of divine frustration: "Do you not know that those who run in a race all run, but one receives the prize? *Run in such a way that you may obtain it . . . I discipline my body and bring it into subjection,* lest, when I have preached to others, I myself should become disqualified."[11]

Somehow, I can't picture Paul settling down into a comfortable church pew. He would keep seeing that prize and start "shadowboxing" in the middle of a service and ruin everything.

God Chasers are so frustrated at times that they make everyone else feel frustrated too. It seems that whatever they have is "catching." The radical God Chasers who become God Catchers have a way of entering our meetings with their hair still smoking from fresh encounters in an upper room somewhere. They are always looking for another worship fire to fan with their passion, so God tends to show up and make it nearly impossible to conduct church as usual.

Some people—the ones who never "catch" God because they refuse to chase Him—constantly ask, "Why can't these radical types just settle down in some deacon position and focus on doing good deeds for God on weekends? They act like this God thing is some full-time vocation, and they are *never* satisfied."

I know of a God Catcher who stated the

Radical God Chasers who become God Catchers have a way of entering our meetings with their hair still smoking from fresh encounters in an upper room somewhere.

answer: "Brethren, I do not count myself to have apprehended; but one thing I do, *forgetting those things which are behind* and *reaching forward* to those things which are ahead, *I press toward the goal for the prize* of the upward call of God in Christ Jesus."[12]

MISSIONARIES TO THE BROKEN LIVE AT FRUSTRATION'S ADDRESS

Why would God have you live at frustration's address? Sometimes the only way He can use you is to send you as a missionary to where the broken are. You have to go through a time of preparation in brokenness.

Moses went *to* the wilderness before he led Israel *through* the wilderness. Jesus endured temptation in His wilderness before He became the answer to the Lord's Prayer by leading us out of temptation and becoming our Daily Bread in the midst of our wilderness.

There are no shortcuts to discipleship. To reach the broken, you must journey through the valley of brokenness and have your "spiritual passport" stamped and verified. Why? The people on your job and in your neighborhood need to see you dealing with the same problems they encounter, but with the joy and strength of the Lord carrying you through while you praise Him.

My suspicion is that when Paul and Silas began to sing praises to God and worship Him in the midnight hour, He left His celestial throne to enter that dark dungeon and sing back to them! "I love you, too, with all My heart."

The significance of living at frustration's address isn't that we are suffering for more of the Lord; it is that we have learned to worship and praise Him regardless of our circumstances or status in life. Our contentment isn't based on what happens to us or what comes our way; it is based solely on His love for us. It is the essence of a "fasted life" devoted to the pursuit of His face.

Once we learn how to worship and sing and chase Him even in a dreary midnight hour, we will accomplish more than just having a "sudden visitation" from Him. When God heard the worship rising from that Philippian prison cell, He came so suddenly that His coming triggered an earthquake that shook chains off more than just Paul and Silas. The Bible says that *all* the prisoners were set free.[13]

You are not singing just for yourself. You are singing for the prostitute down the street. You are singing for the drug addict in the nice house next door who doesn't know how to get out of his self-made hell. You are singing for your neighbor who doesn't know God and doesn't want to live even one more day.

Isn't it interesting that the number of prisoners who get set free in your city may depend on whether you can sing through your pain and midnight desperation? It takes us right back to the shocking truth that church is not about you; church is all about Him!

Paul understood this. He carried a burning burden for the Jewish people in his heart through his life, and he wrote out his "songs" for them: "I tell the truth in Christ, I am not lying, my conscience also bearing me witness in the Holy Spirit, that I have great sorrow and continual grief in my heart. For I could wish that I myself were accursed from Christ for my brethren, my countrymen according to the flesh."[14]

> Isn't it interesting that the number of prisoners who get set free in your city may depend on whether you can sing through your pain and midnight desperation?

NEVER LEAVE A GOD-ENCOUNTER SATISFIED

Paul didn't have a problem with "inward focus." His entire life and ministry exploded outward from his first thirty-second encounter with the manifest presence of God on the Damascus road. He didn't leave that encounter satisfied; he left it eternally and incurably hungry for more of God, along with an unquenchable desire to bring others into His presence—even if it cost him his earthly life!

When was the last time we thought about our "countrymen according to the flesh"? Did we leave our first encounter with God and turn our focus to self or to God and the lost world Jesus came to save?

If you were to lay down this book and say to yourself, "I am so frustrated and hungry for Him that I can't stand it," I would say you are at a good point.

In the natural, most of us eat more than we need because our hunger is greater than our need. Unfortunately we do the opposite when it comes to spiritual things. We "nibble on God" and wind up spiritually malnourished because we prefer to feast on the sweet nothings of spiritual junk food. When hunger is absent from your life in the natural or in the spirit realm, something is probably wrong. Sickness is taking over your body, or apathy is eating away your inner life.

When your hunger is awakened, your health returns. Are you hungry for God? I hope you leave this book feeling miserably and permanently hungry for Him.

Many people do not realize that a dairy farm can continue to produce milk only when the dairyman makes sure his cows—the females in his herd—remain in a virtual state of pregnancy. Without going into the details, a dairy cow produces milk only when she is in the pregnancy or in the nursing cycle. In a way, God keeps the church continuously pregnant with His purposes, and it tends to make those who are serious about Him a bit frustrated at times. It is what Paul meant when he said we are transformed from glory to glory: "But we all, with unveiled face, beholding as in a mirror the glory of the Lord, are being transformed into the same image from glory to glory, just as by the Spirit of the Lord. Therefore, since we have this ministry, as we have received mercy, we do not lose heart."[15]

One time when my wife was pregnant, she bent down to pick something up, and she just toppled over. She was so far along in the pregnancy that her center of gravity had moved farther than her ability to compensate for it.

Some people look at the church and they notice that it seems a bit off center at times. We are stumbling around as if we can't keep our balance. The problem is that we are very pregnant. Our "belly" is taut with the promises of God. We are at that stage of wonderful misery when we know something is coming, but we don't know when or how it will arrive. Now we just have to wait, and in the meantime, we reach for things and nearly lose our balance occasionally. The world looks at us and asks, "What's wrong with the church?"

"Well, you probably have to be a part of the family to understand, but we are pregnant with the purposes of God, and it is almost time to deliver."

> We are at that stage of wonderful misery when we know something is coming, but we don't know when or how it will arrive.

Something wonderful is coming to the frustrated residents of Holy Hunger Street. The God of More Than Enough is coming in the fullness of time, and some divinely discontented God Chasers are about to "catch" God by His design. Something holy and glorious is about to invade and overwhelm your church, your city, and your home. Can you embrace the frustration required for those who wait on the Deity?

Embrace the pregnancy; pull the purposes of God close to you, and don't run from the pain that comes with them. Hold the course, and don't abort what God is trying to do in and through you. God is trying to birth something holy in you. Every earthly mother knows that frustration and even desperation are natural components of the healthy birth process.

FIND DIVINE CONTENTMENT AT FRUSTRATION'S ADDRESS

We need to learn how to leave a worship service hungrier than when we came. If you want to be a God Catcher, you must learn how to live contentedly with divine desperation and holy hunger at frustration's address!

It is a great blessing for me to attend anointed worship services nearly every day of the week, all year long. Yet there are often times when I grow weary of church and reach the point where nothing else but God's manifest presence will satisfy me. I am not a "happy camper" in those seasons of divine discontent; I become a determined God Chaser with a one-track mind and heart. I'm after a God-encounter. My only goal is to capture His heart and find rest in His manifest presence. I refuse to let contentment lull me into a spiritual coma.

> Once repentance prepares you, it is passion that propels you in the chase to catch Him.

Contentment is the ruining of a marriage. If passion ever wanes, then the presence of your spouse may disappear. You must keep the flame of passion alive in a marriage to keep the relationship alive.

Have you ever heard a frustrated mother tell her disobedient child, "I've had about enough of you"? Obviously the mother was referring to the child's behavior, not the child. If a spouse says this about a mate, then the passion is gone from the relationship and must be renewed. Instead of saying, "I've had enough of you," the frustrated partner should say, "I can't wait to see you."

David knew the secret of renewing his passion for God. He wrote, "I was glad when they said to me, 'Let us go into the house of the LORD.'"[16] But it was really to see the "Lord of the house"! He loved to pursue the face of God in passionate worship and intimacy. He did such a good job as a worshiper that we are still scrambling to catch up to his example of uninhibited love and worship.

If there is only one honeymoon in a marriage, it will never last. I'm not referring to a literal trip to a hotel room at a tourist destination. I am saying that if you want a healthy and vibrant marriage, then you must make many trips to the well of passion.

The church needs to rediscover the power of passion for God. When godly passion is birthed in the church, God's presence enters through the door once again. Jesus said, "Nevertheless I have this against you, that you have *left your first love*. Remember therefore from where you have fallen; repent and do the first works, or else I will come to you quickly and remove your lampstand from its place—unless you repent."[17]

> David's radical three risked everything to break through the barriers of Self to bring the king a refreshing drink from the well of the House of Bread.

The process of pursuit begins with "repentance on bended knee," not with religious procedures or proud proclamations of revival. First you enter the "zip code" of God's presence, the realm of repentance and the contrite or humble heart.

As Paul pointed out using his own life as an example, no earthly credentials proclaiming your spiritual excellence will do in His presence.[18] Put them aside when you want access to His presence. The only "master's in divinity" that counts in His presence is the mastery of passionate ministry in humble worship and praise of Him.

Once repentance prepares you, it is passion that propels you in the chase to catch Him. I read about three desperate men who risked their lives to draw water from the well of their king's desire.[19]

They lived in a constant tension of readiness

so they could chase after their king, and they lived to do his slightest will. They happened to overhear him say that he was thirsty for a drink from the well at the House of Bread. The problem was that it was surrounded by a garrison of people called "Wallowing in Self."[20]

Before the king knew it, the radical three risked everything to break through the barriers of Self to bring the king a refreshing drink from the well of the House of Bread. David was the king and the well was in Bethlehem, but doesn't this incident in the Bible speak volumes to the church today?

God still longs for a refreshing drink from the well in the church, the House of Bread He raised up for Himself. It is the only house on earth that has the ability to "feed and refresh God" from its well of worship and praise. The problem is that the well is surrounded by wallowing flesh, and only the fearless can break through it to bring refreshment and rest to the King. It takes a determined God Chaser to deliver what God desires and become a God Catcher.

I want to pray for you one more time about your hunger and desperation level:

> *Father, make us so hungry for Your presence that we are miserable, frustrated, and totally obsessed with You. Cause us to long for You so deeply that we make constant "nagging phone calls" to heaven saying, "Daddy, I want You!" May the pursuit of Your presence become the magnificent obsession of our lives.*
>
> *Impart to us a massive, life-changing, life-disrupting hunger that makes us desperate for You. Set our hearts on fire with passion.*
>
> *Father, break out in churches around the world. Invade churches of every type. Break out in bars, in shopping malls, on farms, in schools, at traffic lights, and at football games. We take the limits off You, Lord, because our hunger knows no limits.*

12

ONLY GOD CHASERS CAN BECOME GOD CATCHERS

WOULD YOU CLIMB A TREE OF DESTINY TO MEET ME?

G OD CHASERS BECOME GOD CATCHERS WHEN THEY begin to measure time in terms of absences from His manifest presence.

A while back I slipped away for a quiet afternoon in between services. I went to one of my favorite coffee shops situated in a shopping mall and settled down "in the zone." (I was just staying in His presence and listening to Him speak to my heart.)

Between sips of strong gourmet coffee, I just let my mind do its thing until I noticed a little boy nearby who was obviously waiting for someone. I was situated on a raised dining area surrounded by a low barrier and some decorative plants, but I could still see him. What caught my attention was the way he kept looking up at me with big puppy-dog eyes.

I tried to appear nonthreatening to him because I didn't want to frighten the little fellow. (I was positive his mother had taught him, "Don't you talk to strangers.")

Finally I said, "Hey, buddy."

He said, "Hi, mister."

"What are you doing?"

"Waiting on my mom," he said.

"Where is she?"

He pointed toward a nearby store and said, "She went in that store and I didn't want to go in there. I just wanted to be out here, so she told me to wait right here."

Somehow I must have "turned on the faucet" of his words because he began to spill out the details of his whole life.

Then he said, "I'm just tired of shopping." A second later he glanced back at the vacant doorway of the store and said, "She said if I'd wait right here, she'd be back."

Something in the tone of his voice told me that he was getting nervous, and I asked, "Has she been gone long?"

He said, "Not really, but kind of." (That is little-boy language for, "I'm going to be brave. I thought I could handle this because I sure didn't want to go in that lingerie store, but I can't see her in there.")

Children don't measure the passage of time the way we do. For a little baby, thirty seconds away from Mommy can seem like eternity. The older we get, the easier it becomes for us to handle separation from our parents—and from God's presence. It just gets harder to recover the "joy of encounter" with Him.

When you play hide-and-seek with a toddler, you could hide in the same place every time and still see the same incredible joy spread over his face when he finds you in your "hiding place." My daughters used to act as if they hadn't seen me in two weeks, even though I'd been hiding only two minutes. Why? Children do not measure time by the ticks of a clock or the forward progress of clock hands or dials. They measure time in terms of absences: "How long has it been since I held my mommy?"

The little boy in the mall was doing his best to be brave, but he sure missed his mother that day. Finally I asked the little fellow, "So you're a

> Children do not measure time by the ticks of a clock or the forward progress of clock hands or dials. They measure time in terms of absences.

little bit worried?" He seemed relieved that somebody had brought it out in the open.

"Yeah, I haven't seen her."

I said, "Are you really worried that she's not coming back?"

He said, "No." Then he tucked his head down and grinned a shy little grin and said, "My mommy would *never* leave me."

"Well, what are you doing while you are waiting?"

He said, "I'm just thinking about stuff."

HE DIDN'T EVEN BOTHER TO SAY "BYE"

I nursed my cup of coffee long enough to at least let him feel that he wasn't totally alone in his faithful wait for Mommy. Every once in a while, I would chat with him through the enclosure and over the decorative bushes until his mom came out of the store. The moment that little boy saw his mother, it was as if he had never even seen me! He didn't even bother to say, "Bye, mister," wave, or glance back in my direction. I couldn't blame him because I feel the same way about my heavenly Daddy.

Time moves slowly when you are hungry to see someone's face *because it is measured in absences.* You just want to be where you will meet the one you long for.

God is omnipresent, meaning He is everywhere all the time. Yet we have also learned from His Word and personal experience that He is able to concentrate His presence from time to time. In that sense, our Father leaves us on this lonely planet called earth from time to time. He says, "I'll be back. Just wait on Me until I come again." Obviously this statement would apply to the second return of Christ to the earth (and I realize there are many different opinions about the details of that return), but I specifically apply it to the times we find ourselves waiting for His *manifest presence* to come among us one more time.

With that little fellow waiting and watching anxiously for his mother in the mall, we see a picture of our own worship and anticipation of our Father's return to our place of waiting and worship. The moment He comes, the instant the Object of our worship comes, we latch on to His glory and press into His presence. We forget to say "bye" to the day's routines, and we often abandon our friendships and break our conversations mid-sentence to exclaim in breathless joy, "It's Him!"

When we wait upon Him in desperate hunger and passion, even the moments of silent waiting are actually a type of worship. We've learned that waiting on God is not "spiritual thumb twiddling" or constantly asking, "I wonder what we're going to do next?" No, it is the art of purposeful anticipation of the next moment. We wait for Him and anticipate His sudden appearing while being consumed with zeal for His presence.

David the psalmist, the brokenhearted sinner and anointed worshiper, wrote, "The LORD is near to those who have a broken heart."[1]

God is attracted to the "pitiful" side of your personality and life. Nothing else interests Him. Your righteousness is as a "filthy rag" in His sight.[2] He is repelled by you at your best, but He is attracted to you in your brokenness.

When problems and pain come your way, turn them into altars. Worship Him over your obstacles, and transform your brokenness into a song of desperation to accelerate the chase for the heart of God.

> Waiting is the
> art of purposeful
> anticipation of
> the next
> moment.

Hang Your Toes Over the Edges of God's Promises

Where do you go when there is nowhere else to go? You hang your toes over the edges of God's promises and "stand still, and see."[3] You may have to worship at "midnight" while you embrace your pain, but the fragrance of your brokenness will draw Him close. I can't tell you that everything is going to be all right because God will not force His will upon the will of men or women. But I can tell you that if you break the alabaster box, *He will come to you.*

Nothing summons the presence of Daddy like a scream from the backyard. When we get older, we usually try to preserve our dignity. We need to discard our dignity so we can regain our intimacy with the Divinity.

In previous writings I said, "Only dead men can really see His face."[4] So the closer you are to death, the closer He is to you. If you can ever "say good-bye to yourself," you can say hello to Him. (Let me warn you that the hardest thing you'll ever do is say good-bye to the tacky trio, "me, myself, and I.")

There is one thing that will cause God to abandon the worship of the archangels in heaven—it is that desperate cry from the "backyard" called earth. Once He hears that cry, once He hears the crash and tinkle of breaking alabaster boxes and the passionate cries of broken hearts, He comes faster than time itself. He won't leave His heavenly throne for just any nonchalant prayer or sound of casual praise. He comes to those whose divine desperation and holy hunger drive them to cry out in childlike frustration, "I'm going to die if I don't have You!" How hungry are you?

Fire without fuel is a smoldering failure waiting to happen.

Every time you gather to worship Him with other believers, remind yourself, "Maybe this is the night. Maybe He will come again and stay this time."

Make sure you come before Him dry, thirsty, and hungry. Your job is to become the fuel of God. Fire without fuel is a smoldering failure waiting to happen, a brief and bright disappointment on the horizon of human hope.

Approach His presence with a burning desire for ignition. I've been told that when John Wesley was asked about the "secret" to his powerful ministry, he said, "I just set myself on fire for God and people come to see me burn."

How dry are you? How hungry are you? How frustrated do you feel right now? Every time you grow weary and frustrated with the painful pursuit of God's presence, remember that frustration is the address to which God sends the anointing. Holy frustration is a characteristic of godly hunger and thirst for God. Be thankful that you are hungry—hunger is the process that keeps your spirit and body alive.

Some people go through life determined to "get along and make do" with whatever comes along. They become living thermometers that merely reflect the ambient temperature of their culture and the people around them. I'm tired of the church being a spiritual thermometer that simply reflects the ambient temperature of society. A thermostat isn't made to merely reflect or measure ambient temperature. It is made to predict and control its surroundings.

A supernatural thermostat, a zealot for the kingdom, says, "I'm going to keep throwing myself on the fire until my passion for His presence draws Him to this place." That is what you and I are supposed to do in our cities and nation. "I know what it looks like out there, but I'm not moved by that. I'm raising the thermostat to move it to the level it is supposed to be."

Turn the Dial of Passion as High as It Will Go!

I pray that someone starts "adjusting the thermostat" in cities around the world. May these desperate "firebrands" turn the dial of passion as high as it will go, saying, "I don't care. I'm not going to stop until the whole city is on fire!" That happens only when people have had a "suddenly," a God-encounter in the temple or an upper room. It happens when people have "waited" on Him long enough to catch their "hair on fire" and have their tongues touched by the fire of God.

If you are frustrated about "church," then you may be getting close to a tree of destiny on the side of life's road. If you can't stand what's going on in your life, then you may be minutes away from a breakthrough. Pray that you will be anything but satisfied.

All I can say is that I have been "smitten of Him," and I hope that I'm so contagious that you catch the same disease. I'm out to make you and those around you "carriers" of the disease of spiritual *dis*-ease and divine desperation. My hope is that in some way I can leave some trail signs or erect a few landmarks to help you find your own way into His presence.

I've learned that if you want to attract His presence, brokenness is His favorite perfume and tears are His favorite anointing. When something happens in the course of life that breaks your heart or bruises your soul, pull the pain to you and offer it to the Lord. There have been times when I felt that I couldn't hurt anymore and live, but suddenly I sensed Him there.

It dawned on me that when that brokenness occurs in my life, He shows up and says, "Oh, I see you've put on My favorite fragrance again." He doesn't revel in our pain or loss, but He does respond to the brokenness and need in our lives.

> Brokenness is His favorite perfume . . . When something happens . . . that breaks your heart or bruises your soul, pull the pain to you and offer it to the Lord.

God doesn't come to you simply because problems come along; He comes because you are *tender*. If you can learn to stay at that tender stage of brokenness *without* the necessity of contrary circumstances, then you will be "falling *on* the Rock" as opposed to having "the Rock fall on *you*."[5] Both create the same fragrance of brokenness, but one is self-induced and the other one is circumstantially induced.

ANY MINUTE NOW HE'S COMING

Now there will be times when circumstances break your heart. It is part of life in a fallen world. We must learn to allow them to create brokenness in our lives and produce an incredible opportunity for divine visitation. Every time something difficult happens in my life that creates deep brokenness and another opportunity to "wait on God," I start saying, *"Any minute now He's coming.* He would never leave me to go through this alone. It won't be long. I'm baptized in brokenness, and I'm going to have an encounter with Him."

Difficult circumstances create brokenness, and He runs to our brokenness. Why do we run *from* what He runs *to*? Point all the pain produced by unfilled broken dreams toward Him. Allow the presence of God to open up new windows for you.

We can never have what we need to have until we can get hungrier than we've been because our capacity for being filled is totally determined by the capacity of our emptiness. We must learn to leave services hungrier than when we came.

The people who seem the hungriest are the same people who know how to *worship Him* in spirit and in truth. They have learned to hunger and thirst for the same One they worship and adore.

When Jesus met the Samaritan woman at the well that day, He had a divine appointment at the well of life. *A thirsty soul was waiting for a miracle.* The twelve professional preachers who followed Jesus returned to the well from the local café and wondered why He didn't want any of the natural food or drink they brought Him. He had been fed by the hunger of the woman at the well, and He satisfied her thirst with living water from the heart of God.

In "good times" (in the relative absence of pain or stressful life challenges), it used to be easier for me to measure the passage of time by my accomplishments, by the upcoming breaks in my schedule, or by highlights of my family calendar such as my wedding anniversary, family birthdays, and the holidays when family and friends get together. *Then I had that God-encounter from which I've never recovered.*

I still love to celebrate important family events and spend time with family members, but since that first point of encounter, I've found myself measuring time in terms of "absences from His manifest presence." I'm convinced that phenomenon isn't unique to me. I've heard too many God Chasers describe the same experience. How do you measure time? David expressed it like this: "I was glad when they said to me, 'Let us go into the house of the LORD.'"[6] Does that mean he would say, "*I was sad* when they said to me, 'You must leave the Lord of the house'"?

Will you be a Mary, a passionate box-breaker bearing the fragrance of brokenness? First, you must abandon the crowd of voices trying to steal or withhold worship from God in the name of preserving man's program. Mary was interested in His presence. She was just glad He was there.

Everyone else wanted to see what he could *get* or gain from Him, but she wanted to see what she could *give* to Him. Church is not what you get out of it; church is what you give to Him.

The Father is bending over the ramparts of

> I've found myself measuring time in terms of "absences from His manifest presence."

heaven. He hears the irresistible crackle and the tinkle of breaking alabaster boxes. Is that the sound of your heart breaking? An incredible fragrance is filling the atmosphere, and I hear the rumors of His sudden approach.

Can you hear the footsteps of Jesus coming as He says, "I smell My favorite fragrance"? He is near to them who are of a broken heart; He can't turn His face away from brokenness.

DID THE FRAGRANCE THAT DREW HIS PRESENCE COME FROM YOU?

Often the presence of God hangs heavy in our prayer rooms and churches, but ten minutes after we leave them, the presence has lifted from us. Are you frustrated with that process?

The secret may be that the fragrance that drew His presence didn't come from *you*. Were you enjoying the fragrance of someone else's brokenness? Perhaps that is why you have nothing to carry home with you once you leave a service.

If you're just enjoying the fragrance of others, you may never know whose brokenness brings fragrance in the room. I can tell you this: God's manifest presence will go home only with the one whose brokenness summoned Him.

It's time to break your alabaster box.

When Mary went home the night after she broke her alabaster box of brokenness over Jesus, she still smelled like Him. When she lay down to sleep, she still smelled like Him. When she got up the next morning, she still smelled like Him.

Are you desperate for the kind of God-encounter that goes with you? This is the key:

you must break your own alabaster box. He won't break it for you; you must break it.

Mary sacrificed her future for His present presence. What would you give to be saturated in His presence for just thirty seconds? It's time to break your alabaster box.

If it doesn't cost you anything, then it's someone else's brokenness. Worship that costs you nothing is momentary, but worship that costs you goes with you.

Mary is at the door, carrying her alabaster box . . .

Blind Bartimaeus smells the dust and hears the clamor of yet another oncoming crowd. Is this the day he receives his sight and sees his Savior?

Isaiah is entering the temple after the death of King Uzziah . . .

Moses is near the end of his first forty years in the wilderness, and a bush is burning with a curious unearthly fire just around the next bend . . .

Perhaps the reputation of these biblical heroes is intimidating to you. Maybe you feel like saying:

"I'm too weak to chase *anybody*, let alone God."

Remember, a baby's cry of weakness can access the strength of the Father faster than the speed of light. If you *never* chase Him, you can *never* catch Him. Besides, your weakness will qualify you for a miracle if you put your hunger and desperation on open display. Put a voice to your frustration and cry out to Him.

Zacchaeus is about to climb the tree of destiny. He has no idea that his earthly wealth will be reduced by the end of the evening meal, nor does he know that his spiritual wealth will reach cosmic proportions once he sheds his pride and climbs a sycamore tree to meet his Master.

It's time for all of us to drop our pride of position and climb the tree of destiny. We can't be late for our divine dinner appointment with the God of our dreams.

Are you desperate for God? It's time to abandon everything that would keep you blind and downtrodden in the dust of your spiritual poverty. Throw off the cloak of man's judgments and religious opinions. Follow the path of blind Bartimaeus. Stand up and let the stench of a life spent begging for the support and approval of man fall away forever.

Earthly brokenness creates heavenly openness. When the fountains of the great deep are broken up, the windows of heaven are opened up: "On that day all the fountains of the great deep were broken up, and the windows of heaven were opened."[7] It's as if I can hear the creaking of the heavenly windows beginning to open. It's time to release the cry God can't deny:

"Daddy, I want *You!*"

ABOUT THE AUTHOR

Tommy Tenney is a God Chaser. Three generations of ministry in his family heritage have given him unique perspectives on the church, leadership, and ministry. He is the founder of The GodChasers.network and is the author of the bestsellers *The God Chasers, God's Favorite House,* and *God's Dream Team.* Tommy and his wife, Jeannie, reside in Louisiana with their three daughters, Tiffany, Natasha, and Andrea. A Yorkie, "Little Romeo," rounds out the Tenney family.

If you have been touched by the message of this book, Tommy and his staff would love to hear from you! You can visit his Web site, write, or call today!

Visit Tommy on the web: www.GodChasers.net
E-mail: GodCatcher@GodChasers.net

Tommy Tenney
The GodChasers.network
P.O. Box 3355
Pineville, LA 71361

Phone: (318) 442-4273
Fax: (318) 442-6884

Notes

Chapter 1

1. See Isaiah 6:1.
2. Tommy Tenney, *The God Chasers* (Shippensburg, PA: Destiny Image Publishers, 1998), p. 2.
3. Ibid., p. 10.
4. See Psalms 10:1; 13:1; 27:9; 44:24; 55:1; 69:17; 88:14; 89:46; 102:2; 104:29; 143:7.
5. Matthew 18:3.
6. Psalm 27:8; Isaiah 55:6.

Chapter 2

1. The "restless remnant" is my term for people who want more from their relationship with God than mere "fire insurance" or entrance to heaven someday when the Lord returns. They know there is more to following Christ than the mere practice of religion. They are the "good soil" Jesus described in His parable of the sower; they are the good stewards who carefully invest God's investment in them to reap a great harvest as described in the parable of the talents. This remnant is the one out of ten lepers who returned to bow at Jesus' feet and thank Him for healing and cleansing his disease. The restless remnant is comprised of "the few, the humble, and the broken" who refuse to bow their knees to false gods, false messiahs, false shepherds, or trivial religious pursuits because they want only to see His face and dwell in His presence. The big problem with this remnant

is that its members aren't easily cataloged, cross-referenced, or "boxed." Their only common characteristic (and the only prerequisite for membership) is their defining hunger for the presence of the living God. Other than that, they include the rich and the poor, the beautiful and the ugly, the powerful and the powerless. You will see blood-washed former prostitutes worshiping Him beside teary-eyed elderly nuns, redeemed bar bouncers, and former Mafia hit men who have been forgiven in Christ.

2. Isaiah 6:1.

3. Isaiah the prophet ministered under the rule of up to five kings of Judah, based in Jerusalem, including Uzziah (also called Azariah), Jotham, Ahaz, and Hezekiah. According to a citation on page 285 in Henry Halley, *Halley's Bible Handbook: New Revised Edition* (Grand Rapids, MI: Zondervan Publishing House, 1973), rabbinic tradition claims that Manasseh, the fifth king in Jerusalem during Isaiah's lifetime, commanded that the prophet be "sawn asunder" after he resisted the king's idolatrous decrees. This may be the martyrdom referred to in Hebrews 11:37.

4. Ibid., p. 285.

5. See 2 Chronicles 26.

6. Isaiah 6:1 KJV.

7. Only Isaiah and God Himself really know how long the prophet stood transfixed in God's manifest presence, but we know from the testimony of others such as Abraham, Moses, and the apostle Paul that it takes only a thirty-second encounter with God's presence to be eternally changed (and to change eternity).

8. Acts 17:27.

9. Glenn Clark, *God's Reach* (St. Paul, MN: Macalester Park Publishing Company, 1951), p. 25.

10. See how Saul sinned against God through presumption and proud disobedience in 1 Samuel 13:8–14.

11. 2 Chronicles 26:5, 16–19, 21, emphasis added.

12. See 2 Samuel 6:6–7. Uzzah's name means "strength" according to James Strong, *Strong's Exhaustive Concordance of the Bible* (Peabody, MA: Hendrickson Publishers, n.d.), Hebrew, #5798, #5797.
13. 2 Timothy 3:5.
14. See Matthew 2:19–21.
15. This is a reference to the human reaction of Peter, James, and John on the Mount of Transfiguration when they saw Jesus revealed in His glory in the presence of Elijah and Moses (Luke 9:32–36). Peter wanted to stop and build tabernacles in honor of the wrong things. The glory on Elijah and Moses didn't come from them—they were merely reflecting the brilliant glory flowing from the King of glory.
16. See Ezekiel 47:5. This is Ezekiel's powerful prophetic vision of the levels of healing and life-giving "water" that flows from the house or dwelling place of God.
17. See Psalm 42:7.
18. Exodus 33:18.
19. See Isaiah 6:1; 9:6, respectively.
20. Psalm 8:4.
21. Tommy Tenney, *God's Favorite House: If You Build It, He Will Come* (Shippensburg, PA: Fresh Bread, an imprint of Destiny Image Publishers, 1999), pp. 114–15.
22. See Colossians 2:15.
23. See Ezekiel 28:12–13, which lists sardius, topaz, diamond, beryl, onyx, jasper, sapphire, turquoise, and emerald stones.
24. See Revelation 21:19–20. It appears that some celestial general stripped Lucifer of his royal jewels at the same time he was stripped of his heavenly name and renamed Satan, the adversary.
25. Tenney, *God's Favorite House*, p. 116.
26. Matthew 18:3, emphasis added.
27. See Isaiah 6:5–7.
28. Halley, *Halley's Bible Handbook*, p. 285.
29. John 12:41.

Chapter 3

1. Luke 9:23.

2. Ezra 3:11–13, emphasis added.

3. Haggai delivered these prophetic words to Zerubbabel, the man who oversaw the actual rebuilding of the temple walls on the relaid foundations described in Ezra 3 (Hag. 2:9). The third verse supports my thinking about the way the older men viewed the new temple: "Who is left among you who saw this temple in its former glory? And how do you see it now? In comparison with it, is this not in your eyes as nothing?" (Hag. 2:3).

4. Amos 9:13.

5. Philippians 2:13.

6. John 15:5.

7. Luke 11:9 AMPLIFIED. A footnote cited for this verse says, "Charles B. Williams, *The New Testament: A Translation*: The idea of continuing or repeated action is often carried by the present imperative and present participles in Greek" (*The Amplified Bible*, expanded edition [Grand Rapids, MI: Zondervan Publishing House, 1987], p. 1178).

8. Psalm 42:1–2.

9. See Genesis 32:24–32.

10. To learn more about this remarkable "God-encounter," read Genesis 32 and then read Chapter 6, "Never Trust Anyone Without a Limp: Wrestling with Divine Destiny," in my book *God's Favorite House: If You Build It, He Will Come*.

11. See Luke 2:25–32.

12. Revelation 1:10–11.

13. See my book *The God Chasers*, Chapter 9, "Dismantle Your Glory," pp. 126–33, for more about Mary's passionate and shameless sacrifice to the Lord in the face of religious hypocrisy and criticism described in Luke 7:36–50 and Mark 14:6, 8–9.

14. See what happens when a nation of people turns from sin to seek Him in 2 Chronicles 7:14.

15. See 2 Corinthians 11:30.
16. See *The God Chasers*, Chapter 10, "Moses' 1,500-Year Pursuit of God's Glory," pp. 139–52, for a detailed look at Moses' determined pursuit of God beyond the grave as described in Exodus 33:18–20, with its fulfillment in Matthew 17:1–3.
17. Acts 15:16–17. This landmark passage in God's Word formed the basis for *God's Favorite House*, a book I wrote on "the worship that God accepts."

Chapter 4

1. Tithes and offerings are good and necessary in the Christian life, but we give them because we *need* to give them to God for our own good. He doesn't need them; He owns the cattle on a thousand hills and knows the exact location of every gold vein and diamond field on the planet. If He didn't, He could simply create more with a word. No, we give to God because *we* need to; but we should never expect our offerings to impress Him. Our best offerings to Him are our words bathed and signed with our passionate hunger.
2. This phrase often speaks of the intimacy of the Communion table when "God and man are sat down" before the elements of bread and the fruit of the vine. Yet it also speaks of those times and places when He literally manifests His presence among living believers in supernatural communion and union of the heart. It is during these times that God "sups" or dines with us—we feast on the bread of His presence and He feasts on our childlike worship, praise, and humble adoration.
3. John 4:42 emphasis added.
4. John 12:21.
5. 1 Corinthians 1:29.
6. Even the sudden visitation of God at Brownsville Assembly of God on Father's Day, 1995, came about not primarily as a result of an evangelist's preaching or of a particular order of service. According

to Pastor John Kilpatrick, a deep longing for more of God's presence and power led him "to a deeper journey of prayer seven years before the revival descended" (John Kilpatrick, *When the Heavens Are Brass: Keys to Genuine Revival* [Shippensburg, PA: Revival Press, an imprint of Destiny Image Publishers, 1997], p. xi). Growing numbers of his congregation began to join him in intercessory prayer in the latter part of that "prayer journey," and God raised the hunger level of that Pensacola, Florida, church to new levels just before His visitation. I have been privileged to minister in the Brownsville meetings, and I can tell you the people there are still seeking Him for *more*.

7. Jesus made it clear that He alone is the doorway to God (John 14:6). The Bible calls Him the "firstborn from the dead" in Colossians 1:18 and Revelation 1:5.

8. This is my paraphrase of Luke 11:52.

9. The Lord pointedly ate with sinners and outcasts (such as tax collectors, non-Jews, repentant prostitutes, and lepers) to the exasperation of the religiously bigoted Pharisees. See Matthew 9:10–13; 11:19; and Luke 15:1–10.

10. The term "bread of His presence" is explained in this brief passage from my book *The God Chasers*, Chapter 2: "No Bread in the 'House of Bread,'" p. 19: "Bread has always been the one thing historically that was an indicator of His presence. We find in the Old Testament that bread in the form of showbread was in the Holy Place. It was called 'the bread of the Presence' (Num. 4:7 NRSV). Showbread might better be interpreted as 'show up bread,' or in the Hebraic terms, 'face bread.' It was a heavenly symbol of God Himself."

11. Please understand that my distaste for man's programs and religious rituals is directed toward *empty* actions, patterns, and methodologies designed to fill the empty void caused by God's obvious absence from man's proceedings. At times, I have seen God's presence permeate "high church" services that were based on ancient church rituals. On the other hand, I also have attended some seemingly

unprogrammed services in nondenominational churches that were as rigid and lifeless as any I have ever seen. The crucial question is this: Whom are you hungry for? Are you seeking Him, or will you be satisfied with the solace of your ritual or ritualistic patterns of worship minus His presence? You get what you seek.

12. See Acts 9:1–6.
13. I refer briefly to the Lord's triumphal entry into Jerusalem in my book *The God Chasers*, on pp. 17 and 18 of Chapter 2, "No Bread in the 'House of Bread.'"
14. See Matthew 21:1–16 and John 12.

Chapter 5

1. Matthew 18:3.
2. See Revelation 3:17.
3. Luke 19:1–6.
4. See Romans 3:23.
5. Paraphrased from Jeremiah 29:11.
6. Bartimaeus is mentioned by name in the account found in Mark 10:46–52.
7. The name Bartimaeus is of Chaldean origin, which is similar in some respects to Hebrew. *Bar* means "son," and *Timaeus* means "unclean, defiled, polluted," according to *Strong's Exhaustive Concordance of the Bible*, Bartimaeus (Greek #924, Hebrew #1247 and #2931).
8. This view was explained in detail and supported by Dr. Merrill C. Tenney in the *New Testament Survey* (Grand Rapids, MI: Wm. B. Eerdmans Publishing Co., 1961), pp. 155–57.
9. Mark 10:46–48.
10. Adapted and "personalized" from Acts 17:27 KJV.
11. Isaiah 55:6.

Chapter 6

1. Ephesians 2:6.
2. See 1 John 4:20.
3. See John 21:25.
4. See John 11:3–15.
5. See Hebrews 13:8.
6. John 11:24.
7. See John 11:25.
8. Isaiah 40:31.
9. Halley, *Halley's Bible Handbook,* p. 561, says pentecost fell on the tenth day after Jesus' ascension to heaven, and the fiftieth day after His resurrection from the dead.
10. See Acts 1–2.
11. See 1 Corinthians 15:6.
12. Luke 24:49. According to Paul the apostle in 1 Corinthians 15:6, the resurrected Christ appeared to more than five hundred witnesses "at once." Some people believe this describes the number of people who saw Jesus ascend to heaven after issuing His command that they "tarry" in Jerusalem.
13. See Acts 1:13–15; 2:1–3.
14. Matthew 22:37.
15. See 2 Timothy 3:15–17 (concerning God's Word) and Ephesians 4:8–12 (concerning God's equipping or leadership [*doma*] gifts to the church).
16. See Romans 7:6. The context is the difference between the rigid Mosaic and Levitical Law passed down from the past and expanded by the Pharisees and the law of the Spirit received through Christ. We have nearly reconstructed the dogma of "salvation by works" that Jesus came to replace or supplant. We are saved through *relationship* with our Redeemer, not through works. We must study and obey God's Word to grow and do the work of the kingdom, but it is

reduced to mere "works of man" without an abiding *intimate relationship* with God. If God wanted only Bible automatons who religiously observed every jot and tittle of His Word, then He wouldn't have endured the sorrow of the Cross. He already had that in the Pharisees. *He wanted more*—and so should we.

17. See John 1:14.

18. See Exodus 17:8–15.

19. Song entitled "Waiting on You," written by Clint Brown (BMI) and Sheryl Brady (ASCAP). Copyright Registration #PA2368984. © 1998 Tribe Music Group (Admin. PYPO Publishing), BMI. © 1998 Judah First Music.

Chapter 7

1. God first revealed Himself as *El Shaddai* to Abraham in Genesis 17:1. Dr. C. I. Scofield's footnote on the divine name in this verse, printed in the *Scofield Reference Bible* (New York: Oxford University Press, 1967), says, "*El Shaddai* is the name of God which sets Him forth primarily as the strengthener and satisfier of His people. It is to be regretted that *Shaddai* was translated 'Almighty.' The primary name, *El* or *Elohim*, sufficiently signifies almightiness. 'All-sufficient' would far better express the characteristic use of the name in Scripture." I have heard others translate this name to mean the "God of More Than Enough." The most significant outpouring of His filling upon human emptiness is described in Acts 2, when the Holy Spirit descended on the 120 on the day of pentecost.

2. Psalm 34:17–18.

3. Matthew 5:6.

4. 2 Kings 4:1–3, emphasis added.

5. 2 Kings 4:4–7, emphasis added.

6. Judges 2:18; Psalm 101:5.

7. James 5:11 KJV.

8. Hebrews 7:25.

9. James 5:16.

10. "Casual nibblers" tend to major on "the truth of where God has been." It causes us to "live with less than God's best." For more on this subject, see my book *God's Favorite House*, pp. 38–39, in Chapter 3, "Opening Heaven and Closing the Gates of Hell."

11. See the description of the church of Laodicea in Revelation 3:14–19.

12. See Mark 6:48–49.

13. See Joshua 10:12–14, where God made the sun and moon stand still at Joshua's request during a battle for the occupation of the promised land.

14. Jesus resurrected the son of the widow of Nain in Luke 7:11–16, and God delivered Queen Esther, Mordecai, and the Jewish people from wicked Haman in Esther 4:1–3; 6:7–10; and 7:9, respectively.

15. See Isaiah 59:19.

16. 2 Timothy 3:7.

17. Matthew 5:6, emphasis added.

18. Matthew 5:6.

19. See Acts 9:1–5.

20. God attaches tremendous importance to the covenantal principle of the "middle ground." For a more substantial explanation of this place where God and man meet, refer to Part I: "Preserving the Middle Ground," in *Answering God's Prayer: A Personal Journal with Meditations from "God's Dream Team"* (Ventura, CA: Regal Books, an imprint of Gospel Light, 2000), pp. 13–24.

21. Matthew 18:20.

Chapter 8

1. 1 Samuel 3:10.

2. See 2 Corinthians 3:18.

3. See Chapter 6, "How to Handle the Holy," in *The God Chasers*, pp. 83–99, for an in-depth discussion of David's tragic journey from Nachon's threshing floor to Obed-Edom's house, and his remarkable

second journey from Obed-Edom's house to the "tabernacle of David" in Jerusalem.

4. See Philippians 2:7.

5. Tenney, *God's Favorite House,* p. 36, in Chapter 3, "Opening Heaven and Closing the Gates of Hell."

6. See Ephesians 2:13; Hebrews 13:12–15; Romans 12:1.

7. Genesis 22:8 KJV.

8. Strong, *Strong's Exhaustive Concordance of the Bible,* Jehovah Jireh (Hebrew #3070).

9. *God's Favorite House,* pp. 48–49, in Chapter 4, "Building a Mercy Seat."

10. See 2 Kings 4:8.

11. 2 Kings 4:15–17.

12. See Ephesians 2:14.

13. See Matthew 8:20; Luke 9:58.

14. 2 Kings 4:32–37.

15. Matthew 5:3, 6.

16. See Luke 9:62.

17. T. F. Tenney and Tommy Tenney, *Secret Sources of Power: Rediscovering Biblical Power Points* (Shippensburg, PA: Fresh Bread, an imprint of Destiny Image Publishers, 2000), pp. 121–22.

18. See John 3:6–8.

19. Tommy Tenney, *God's Dream Team: A Call to Unity* (Ventura, CA: Regal Books, a division of Gospel Light, 1999), p. 122, in Chapter 8, "The Supernatural Potential of Unity." This book focuses on the only unanswered prayer of Jesus: "That they may be one." It is also the only prayer of God that only man has the power to answer.

20. See Matthew 18:19–20.

21. See John 13:35.

22. Romans 12:18.

23. This quote comes from an interview of six elderly prayer veterans of the New Hebrides revival in England. The audiotape is titled "Revival Fire." It is not copyrighted, and it is available through the

GodChaser.network at P.O. Box 3355, Pineville, Louisiana 71361. You may also call the ministry at 318-442-4273, or visit our Web site at www.GodChasers.net.

Chapter 9

1. See Song 2:14 KJV.

2. See Ephesians 2:14.

3. God "repented" three times in one chapter alone. See Jeremiah 26:3, 13, 19 KJV.

4. Song 2:14 KJV, emphasis added.

5. See John 4:23.

6. Ezekiel 14:14, emphasis added.

7. Jeremiah 15:1, emphasis added.

8. Genesis 6:8.

9. Daniel 10:12–14, 19, emphasis added.

10. See Hebrews 7:25–26.

11. Job 42:7–8, emphasis added.

12. Luke 23:34.

13. Numbers 16:45.

14. Numbers 16:48.

15. Exodus 33:17–18, emphasis added.

16. Tenney, *The God Chasers*, p. 139, in Chapter 10, "Moses' 1,500-Year Pursuit of God's Glory." This entire chapter is devoted to Moses' intense desire for more of God than he experienced in the cloud of glory on Mount Sinai and in the tabernacle of the wilderness. God told Moses that no man could see His glory and live, so Moses waited fifteen hundred years to see God's glory revealed in God the Son on the Mount of Transfiguration in Matthew 17:1–3. Only dead men can see His face.

17. Strong, *Strong's Exhaustive Concordance of the Bible*, Samuel (Hebrew #8050).

18. See 1 Samuel 1:9–20.

19. See 1 Samuel 2:18; 3.

20. 1 Samuel 3:19, emphasis added.

21. No one but God knows the exact number of years that passed between the lives of Noah and Daniel (the earliest and more recent, respectively, of the five men listed by the prophets). H. H. Halley estimated that Noah lived around 2400 B.C. (*Halley's Bible Handbook*, p. 34). Daniel was a contemporary of Ezekiel, and he arrived in Babylon around 605 B.C. according to *Eerdman's Handbook to the Bible* (ed. David Alexander and Pat Alexander [Grand Rapids, MI: William B. Eerdman's Publishing Company, 1973], p. 430).

Chapter 10

1. We know Abram was eighty-six years old when Ishmael was born (Gen. 16:16), and he was one hundred years old when Isaac was born (Gen. 17–18; 21:5). The day Ishmael and Hagar were ejected from Abraham's household, we know Ishmael was at least fourteen years old.

2. Genesis 21:17, emphasis added.

3. See Luke 18:9–14.

4. This is my abbreviated version of Exodus 3:7–8.

5. Psalm 51:16–17, emphasis added.

6. See Ephesians 2:13–14.

7. John 2:17.

8. Hosea 14:2.

9. Matthew 12:35.

10. This is a reference to the three mighty men of King David who overheard David say to himself, "Oh, that someone would give me a drink of the water from the well of Bethlehem, which is by the gate!" (2 Sam. 23:15). They immediately broke through the lines of the Philistine army that was camped around the well and drew water from it for King David. God longs to drink from our sacrifice of praise and worship, but very few of us are willing to risk everything to quench God's thirst.

11. I say "thirty seconds" because that is the approximate length of time it takes to read the scriptural transcript of the conversation between Saul and God recorded in Acts 9:1–30 and Galatians 1:12–18.

12. Philippians 1:21–23.

13. Revelation 3:15–19, emphasis added.

Chapter 11

1. Let me make it clear that being a "spiritual traveler in transit" does *not* mean we do not have a fixed local church home. Part of "chasing God" includes submitting to His Word, the work of the Holy Spirit, and the authority of church leaders ordained and anointed by God to equip us for the work of the ministry. God does more than work with individual believers—most of the New Testament Epistles and the book of Revelation were addressed to churches, not to individuals. *For the record*: Chase God, worship Him in unity with other saints in a local congregation of believers, submit to the spiritual leaders God places over you, and walk in unity. That is the surest path to offering an acceptable sacrifice of praise to Him with your life.

2. See Psalm 51:17.

3. See Philippians 2:13.

4. See John 12:32.

5. Matthew 22:37, emphasis added.

6. See Acts 16.

7. Jesus said as much in Matthew 5:45.

8. See Psalm 34:18.

9. Acts 16:6–10, emphasis added.

10. Philippians 4:11–12, emphasis added.

11. 1 Corinthians 9:24, 27, emphasis added.

12. Philippians 3:13–14, emphasis added.

13. See Acts 16:26.

14. Romans 9:1–3.

15. 2 Corinthians 3:18–4:1.
16. Psalm 122:1.
17. Revelation 2:4–5, emphasis added.
18. See Philippians 3:4–8.
19. See the story of King David and his three "mighty men" in 2 Samuel.
20. According to Strong, *Strong's Exhaustive Concordance of the Bible*, the Hebrew meaning of *Bethlehem* is "House of Bread" (Hebrew #1035), and an interpretation of the root Hebrew word (*palash*) for Philistine (*Pelishtiy*) is "Wallowing in Self" (Hebrew #6429, #6428).

Chapter 12

1. Psalm 34:18.
2. See Isaiah 64:6.
3. See Exodus 14:13.
4. Tenney, *The God Chasers*, pp. 51–66, in Chapter 4, "Dead Men See His Face"; *God's Favorite House*, p. 100, in Chapter 7, "Spiritual Pornography or Spiritual Intimacy?"
5. See 1 Peter 2:7–8.
6. Psalm 122:1.
7. Genesis 7:11. This Old Testament reference to the windows of heaven opening up speaks of judgment, but it also gives us a powerful picture of the way God pours out His Spirit and His blessings on repentant hearts and nations. The flood begins when the "fountains of the great deep are broken up." Elsewhere God's Word speaks of His coming this way: "His going forth is established as the morning; He will come to us like the rain, like the latter and former rain to the earth" (Hos. 6:3).

GodChasers.network is the ministry of Tommy and Jeannie Tenney. Their heart's desire is to see the presence and power of God fall—not just in churches, but on cities and communities all over the world.

How to contact us:

By Mail:

GodChasers.network
P.O. Box 3355
Pineville, Louisiana 71361
USA

By Phone:

Voice:	318.44CHASE (318.442.4273)
Fax:	318.442.6884
Orders:	888.433.3355

By Internet:

E-mail:	GodChaser@GodChasers.net
Website:	www.GodChasers.net

Join Today

When you join the **GodChasers.network** we'll send you a free teaching tape!

If you share in our vision and want to stay current on how the Lord is using GodChasers.network, please add your name to our mailing list. We'd like to keep you updated on what the Spirit is saying through Tommy. We'll also send schedule updates and make you aware of new resources as they become available.

Sign up by calling or writing to:

Tommy Tenney
GodChasers.network
P.O. Box 3355
Pineville, Louisiana 71361-3355
USA

318-44CHASE (318.442.4273)
or sign up online at http://www.GodChasers.net/lists/

We regret that we are only able to send regular postal mailings to US residents at this time. If you live outside the US you can still add your postal address to our mailing list—you will automatically begin to receive our mailings as soon as they are available in your area.

E-mail Announcement List

If you'd like to receive information from us via e-mail, just provide an e-mail address when you contact us and let us know that you want to be included on the e-mail announcement list!

AUDIOTAPE ALBUMS BY

Tommy Tenney (signature)

FANNING THE FLAMES
(audiotape album) $20 plus $4.50 S&H

Tape 1 — The Application of the Blood and the Ark of the Covenant: Most of the churches in America today dwell in an outer-court experience. Jesus made atonement with His own blood, once for all, and the veil in the temple was rent from top to bottom.

Tape 2 — A Tale of Two Cities—Nazareth & Nineveh: What city is more likely to experience revival: Nazareth or Nineveh? You might be surprised....

Tape 3 — The "I" Factor: Examine the difference between *ikabod* and *kabod* ("glory"). The arm of flesh cannot achieve what needs to be done. God doesn't need us; we need Him.

KEYS TO LIVING THE REVIVED LIFE
(audiotape album) $20 plus $4.50 S&H

Tape 1 - Fear Not: To have no fear is to have faith, and that perfect love casts out fear, so we establish the trust of a child in our loving Father.

Tape 2 - Hanging in There: Have you ever been tempted to give up, quit, and throw in the towel? This message is a word of encouragement for you.

Tape 3 - Fire of God: Fire purges the sewer of our souls and destroys the hidden things that would cause disease. Learn the way out of a repetitive cycle of seasonal times of failure.

NEW!
GOD'S DREAM TEAM AUDIO SERIES
(audiotape album) $20 plus $4.50 S&H

Only we can answer the only unanswered prayer of Jesus. "That they may be one!" This collection contains three of Tommy's messages on unity.

Video by Tommy Tenney

TURNING ON THE
LIGHT OF THE GLORY
(video) $20 plus $4.50 S&H

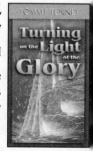

Tommy deals with turning on the light of the glory and presence of God, and he walks us through the necessary process and ingredients to potentially unleash what His Body has always dreamed of.

Fuel for the Pursuit

Resources Available

Tommy Tenney has touched the heart of a generation who crave for an encounter with their Lord. The passion of his heart, captured in his writings, has ignited a flame of godly pursuit across this world.

The Daily Chase offers to you the best of those writings. Each day there awaits for you a fresh encounter with the One you long for.

This first printing includes a sample God Chaser Worship CD enclosed in the back of the book. It includes:

- Sample songs from Jeannie Tenney's album "Holy Hunger"

  Sample songs from a NEW God Chaser worship album

  Sample video clips from the accompanying music video

Elegant Case Bound Edition, $19.00

To order any of the products listed on these pages,
receive information concerning the ministry of Tommy Tenney,
or to join the GodChasers.network, please contact:

GodChasers.network
P.O. Box 3355
Pineville, LA 71361
318-44CHASE (318.442.4273)
888.433.3355
Fax: 318.442.6884
www.GodChasers.net
GodChaser@GodChasers.net

Run With Us!

Become a GodChasers.network Monthly Seed Partner

Two men, a farmer and his friend, were looking out over the farmer's fields one afternoon. It was a beautiful sight—it was nearly harvest time, and the wheat was swaying gently in the wind. Inspired by this idyllic scene, the friend said, "Look at God's provision!" The farmer replied, "You should have seen it when God had it by Himself!"

This humorous story illustrates a serious truth. Every good and perfect gift comes from Him: but we are supposed to be more than just passive recipients of His grace and blessings. We must never forget that only God can cause a plant to grow—but it is equally important to remember that *we are called to do our part in the sowing, watering, and harvesting.*

When you sow seed into this ministry, you help us reach people and places you could never imagine. The faithful support of individuals like you allows us to send resources, free of charge, to many who would otherwise be unable to obtain them. Your gifts help us carry the Gospel all over the world—including countries that have been closed to evangelism. Would you prayerfully consider partnering with us? As a small token of our gratitude, our Seed Partners who send a monthly gift of $20 or more receive a teaching tape every month. This ministry could not survive without the faithful support of partners like you!

Stand with me now—so we can run together later!

In Pursuit,

Tommy Tenney
& The GodChasers.network Staff

Become a Monthly Seed Partner by calling or writing to:

Tommy Tenney/GodChasers.network
P.O. Box 3355
Pineville, Louisiana 71361-3355
318.44CHASE (318.442.4273)